The

CROWN

and the

ESTABLISHMENT

George IV. A Voluptuary under the Horrors of Digestion, by James Gillray

The

CROWN

and the

ESTABLISHMENT

★

KINGSLEY MARTIN

★

HUTCHINSON OF LONDON

HUTCHINSON & CO. (*Publishers*) LTD
178–202 Great Portland Street, London, W.1

London Melbourne Sydney
Auckland Bombay Toronto
Johannesburg New York

First published May 1962
Second impression June 1962

© Kingsley Martin 1962

This book has been set in Times New Roman type face. It has been printed in Great Britain by The Anchor Press, Ltd., in Tiptree, Essex, on Smooth Wove paper and bound by Taylor Garnett Evans & Co., Ltd., in Watford, Herts

To my colleagues

John Freeman
Norman MacKenzie
& Paul Johnson

CONTENTS

ILLUSTRATIONS

LINE-DRAWINGS

ACKNOWLEDGMENTS

I cannot hope to acknowledge my debt to all those who have helped me by discussing the material of this book. Some of them had special knowledge of the working of our monarchical system and of the personalities involved. Mr. L. J. Sharpe, of the London School of Economics and Political Science, has done much invaluable work for me especially in exploring the little-known history of the republican movement in the nineteenth century. Dr. Bernard Crick has most generously found time during the academic term to read the proofs, and has made many important suggestions, some of which I have gladly accepted; others, it is only fair to him to say, I have not been persuaded to follow. To Mr. Paul Johnson, who read the manuscript at an earlier stage and called my attention to sources I had overlooked, and to Professor W. A. Robson, Dr. Anthony Storr and Mr. Sydney Jacobson who have made most valuable suggestions, I owe a special debt. None of these is, of course, in any way responsible for my opinions or for any errors that may have crept in.

I am also grateful to Miss Dorothy Woodman who helped me at various stages, to Mrs. June Newfield, who checked errors in references and quotations, and to Miss Edith M. Horsley of the Hutchinson Publishing Group whose care, patience and indefatigable industry in producing the book have gone far beyond my previous experience of the publishing profession.

I should perhaps add that a small book I wrote on the *Magic of Monarchy* in 1936 has been long out of print as well as out of date. Some chapters of this book have drawn on the earlier one, but this is an entirely new book.

ACKNOWLEDGMENTS

The author thanks the following publishers for permission to quote from the works mentioned: Emrys Hughes *Keir Hardie* (George Allen & Unwin Ltd.), H.R.H. The Duke of Windsor *A King's Story: Memoirs of H.R.H. The Duke of Windsor* (Cassell & Co. Ltd. and Putnam's Sons, New York), Richard Hoggart *The Uses of Literacy* (Chatto & Windus Ltd.), Dermot Morrah *The Work of the Queen* (William Kimber & Co. Ltd.), John W. Wheeler-Bennett *King George VI, his life and reign* and Arthur Ponsonby *Henry Ponsonby, Queen Victoria's Private Secretary: his life from his letters* (Macmillan & Co. Ltd.), an American Resident *The Twilight of the British Monarchy* (Secker & Warburg, Ltd.), and to the present Lord Esher for permission to quote from *Journals and Letters of Reginald Viscount Esher, Volume II* edited by Maurice V. Brett (Nicholson & Watson, Ltd.). The author also thanks William Heinemann Ltd. for permission to reproduce the cartoons by Sir Max Beerbohm, from *Things New and Old* and *Fifty Caricatures*.

1

REPRESENTATIVE MONARCHY

'*There will soon be only five kings left—the Kings of England, Diamonds, Hearts, Spades and Clubs.*'—King Farouk to Lord Boyd-Orr in Cairo, 1951

'*This country and Commonwealth last Tuesday were not far from the Kingdom of Heaven.*'—Archbishop of Canterbury on the Coronation of Elizabeth II

'*The great majority of the human race, which since 1917 has been shedding Kings with delight and abandon, is said to be doing violence to its essential nature.*'—*Daily Worker*, 30 May 1953

'*I have seen a number of names suggested for our new princess, the daughter of the Duke and Duchess of Kent. Mary, Marina, Helen, Alice have been suggested. In my opinion, none of these sufficiently marks the extraordinary miracle of a royal birth in a time of great national stress.*'—Letter to *Observer*, 3 Jan. 1937

MONARCHY in Britain, as King Farouk's quip suggests, stands in a class by itself, uniquely popular and secure. Outside Europe the type of revolution that made Farouk a fugitive has become everyday news. Inside Europe only six monarchies are left. In Greece and Belgium the crown seems precariously poised. The unpretentious monarchs of Scandinavia and the Low Countries are respectfully accepted by their sober subjects. They go out shopping like other mortals without being mobbed by sight-seers or surrounded by photographers; their homes are not besieged, as Buckingham Palace is, by crowds who gather outside it even when no royal personages are in residence.

In short, Scandinavian countries are republics which find it convenient to maintain hereditary presidents—which is what liberal theorists not long ago took also to be the reality of monarchy in Britain.

This commonsense attitude to the throne is now out of fashion in Britain. A glorified, religious view of royalty is the vogue. The Queen is not allowed to wear a crown; nothing less than a halo will suffice. But the halo is neon-lighted—a combination which seems to make the worst of both worlds, the divine and the secular. This unreal light is reflected on all members of the royal family. Writers and speakers change gear every time they mention royalty; their reverent phraseology makes the innumerable books about royal personages astonishing to foreign readers who do not share our novel habit of simultaneously staring and genuflecting.

Officially the Monarchy is treated as sacrosanct, beyond criticism and regarded as essential for national safety. Many tribes maintain such taboos and appoint some person or institution to preserve them intact. The keeper of the British conscience is the B.B.C., which does not permit free speech about religion or monarchy. Debates about Christianity do sometimes take place as a concession to that large majority which, according to the Churches' own admission, are not believers and, therefore, presumably, not usually interested in the numerous religious services that punctuate B.B.C. programmes. But about monarchy the taboo is absolute. The Queen, unlike God, is not even an occasional subject of B.B.C. debate. Broadcasters may argue about socialism, birth control and even homosexuality, but I do not recall republicanism being discussed or even mentioned on the B.B.C. British monarchy is never criticized. This is a remarkable change. A century ago courage was necessary to question the literal truth of the first chapter of Genesis, to doubt the Virgin Birth or discuss problems of sex. The throne on the other hand was frankly criticized in the press and on platforms. In the twentieth century anyone can question the divinity of Christ, but no one attributes faults to the royal family.

Mr. Dermot Morrah, the most eloquent and intimately

informed of the Queen's biographers,[a] argues that the British Monarchy is not to be regarded as an antiquated form of government tolerated in spite of having lost its political importance. On the contrary: 'In its deeper meaning for the British peoples it is scarcely a system of government at all. It is their way of life. As such, it is always popular, it is always changing and always the same; it is always up to date.' Even in days when we have learnt to 'disentangle magic from science and metaphor from thought' there remains in ordinary people an inner craving for a monarch who represents not part but the whole of society. In Britain we have been lucky enough to maintain, with only one instructive lapse in the seventeenth century, a continuity of this basic institution. At the apex of our society stands a representative personality who is not, like a president, a political choice, but the 'embodiment of the whole life of the people; she presides indeed over its political action, but only because politics are one of the necessary departments of life, and of all departments she is the head'.[b]

Mr. Morrah grows more mystical when he approaches the Queen's influence abroad. She is, he says, a symbol, but more than a symbol; she stands

'peculiarly for the idea that the ultimate reality in corporate life—at the heart of what sometimes seems the chilly and soulless machinery of the modern state—is not an abstraction, but a human being of like passions with ourselves. Because she is not a symbol but a person she can, as she moves about her dominions, bring the representation of the whole into direct contact with every part. Wherever she goes, that spot is momentarily the centre of the Commonwealth, and the soldier on parade, the artisan at his bench, the nurse by the bedside and the patient under her care are enabled to feel themselves exalted by the recognition of their place in a world-wide family and a vast design.

Mr. Morrah is doing no more than building up, with style and enthusiasm, a theory of monarchy that has been recently advanced by many less subtle writers. Extravagant views of monarchy are usually expressed at coronations. So notably rational a prelate as Archbishop Temple, for instance, declared that at his coronation George V became the 'incarnation of his people', a phrase which might at first suggest that the King was a scapegoat who bore in his royal person the sins of the people and whose ritual death would be a condition of their prosperity. Bishop Blunt, later,to become famous for a comment that precipitated the abdication crisis, put forward a stranger theory. He opposed the suggestion that any free churchman should take part in the coronation ceremony on the ground that it would be rendered inefficacious unless exclusively solemnized by an archbishop. Its 'benefits' would be impaired by a wrong ritual—a doctrine similar to that of South Sea islanders who regard a coronation as a magic rite that confers on the king the power to control the winds and the rain.

It was not, however, until the accession of Elizabeth II that a sustained effort was made to represent the coronation as a sacrament in which all the population are simultaneously communicants. The development of mass communication by television, the films and the mass-circulation press vastly increased the opportunities of thus improving the occasion. The usually sober *Times* wrote:

> 'Today's sublime ceremonial is in form, and in common view, a dedication of the State to God's service through the prayers and benedictions of the Church. That is a noble conception, and of itself makes every man and woman in the land a partaker in the mystery of the Queen's anointing. But the Queen also stands for the soul as well as for the body of the Commonwealth. In her is incarnate on her Coronation the whole of society, of which the State is no more than a political manifestation. . . .'

Television, we were told by many authorities, made it possible for the entire population to obtain spiritual benefit from the Abbey ceremony. Our family lives were renewed, purified and made fit for national service by this act of dedication. Writers traced the details of the coronation ceremony far back into history; they analysed the traditional significance of the sword, the sceptre and the orb; the various ritual changes of costume and the mysterious words about Melchizedek, the High Priest. Sociologists suggested that moral values, generally accepted in our society, were being reaffirmed in this act of national communion. Prisoners in a Corrective Training Centre were reported to have gained great spiritual benefit from seeing the coronation on television; some writers even appeared to believe that the present monarch would herself exercise the power once symbolized by the sceptre and the sword. A cleric declared that the coronation was a 'miracle which might save civilization', and another, that 'God rarely intervenes in history, but the few occasions when He does are, as one would expect, among the greatest events recorded in its pages.'[d]

The exuberant morass of verbiage about the new Elizabethan Age symbolized by the accession of the young Queen and the simultaneous conquest of Everest reached a point of extravagance which put *The Times* on its guard. 'The Elizabethan Age', it said, 'is in danger of becoming an incantation, a magician's hey presto, as if the nation's new stature could be established merely by proclaiming it.'

There have been three main periods in the development of monarchical institutions in this country since the seventeenth century. The British people have not habitually displayed reverence towards their kings and queens. Three hundred years ago we rid ourselves of the concept of Divine Right which had been invented to justify Renaissance monarchs, who, as heads of national states, transferred to themselves the physical and spiritual powers which the Emperor and Pope had sought to exercise over medieval Christendom. In the eighteenth, nineteenth and twentieth centuries monarchy was similarly demoted throughout Europe; kings who attempted to maintain power, or even to hold on to significant remnants of it, lost their thrones and commonly their lives. Before the middle of this century the process of dethroning absolutism in Europe was complete. A few nimble monarchs retained office by surrendering power. Where they failed to adjust themselves to the changes which everywhere spread from the French Revolution, they were discarded. No one sheds tears for kaisers, tsars and sultans or defends the pretensions of absolutism; where the monarchy was identified with an intolerable regime, revolutionaries, and eventually reformers too, were driven to republicanism.

It seems clear that when the personal and public character of the monarch conforms to the appropriate pattern, there is a natural tendency, which propaganda can easily exploit, to see in him the ideal personification of those qualities which are most admired in contemporary society. In the sixteenth century Tudor despotism was welcomed because it guaranteed order after the baronial wars, secured the nation against foreign enemies and gave the emergent middle class the prospect of stability and riches. In the seventeenth and eighteenth centuries Britain needed a constitutional monarchy to end religious struggle and preserve the new structure of society in which traders, merchants and the new industrialists could exploit the enlarged possibilities of wealth; this was achieved without depriving the aristocracy and gentry of their political power. In the nineteenth century, despite 'no popery' scares, the scarlet woman had ceased to terrify and the acceptance of the democratic idea forbade the public exercise of royal authority. Though the Georges had made the Crown excessively unpopular, Britain was still just—and only just—prepared to accept the Monarchy, but, as the Liberal theorists who dominated British thought made clear, only on specific conditions. Political leaders were now elected and responsible. The Monarchy had become a survival to be maintained, if at all, as a useful constitutional device and the focus of national loyalty. The conditions were that it played no personal part in the political battle and that the character of the monarch could be respected. When at last the public was sure that these two conditions were fulfilled—and that was not until the later part of the century—only then could the politically conscious democracy allow itself to indulge its natural capacity for devotion to an idealized personality.

In Britain, until the third quarter of Queen Victoria's reign, the assumption that democracy logically and necessarily implied republicanism generally held the field. From the time when King George III's distasteful sons approached the throne, monarchy was unpopular; it was regarded by the politically conscious working class and the radical section of the middle class as a remnant of medievalism which, like the House of Lords and other traditional survivals, would disappear with the growth of popular government. Until the last quarter of the century Queen Victoria seemed likely to be the last British monarch; highly respectable Liberals, like John Bright, Sir Charles Dilke, Joseph Chamberlain and John Morley, deprecated as unchivalrous anything like personal criticism of the Queen, but they were not prepared to hold that her scapegrace son Edward should succeed her.

The second period begins with the growth of imperialism in the last quarter of the century. In her old age Queen Victoria, brought from retirement by the skill and flattery of Disraeli, became the adored symbol of domestic virtue and imperial greatness. When Edward VII came to the throne, he proceeded with caution and never flouted the Constitution, which his mother, as only her advisers knew in her lifetime, had often felt at liberty to do. Edward was well aware that monarchy had become an anomaly in democracy and understood the lesson of the unsuccessful rising against the Tsar in 1905. Like Lord Esher, his confidential adviser, he was alarmed at the growth of 'continental socialism'. Towards the end of his life he betrayed his fears for the future by introducing his son, afterwards George V, as the future 'last King of England'.[e] Such thoughts also haunted the mind of George V; a guileless and conscientious monarch, he was always anxious to do his duty and by so doing to strengthen the position of the Crown, at home and especially in the Commonwealth. He was immensely successful, and in the later part of his reign was both surprised and touched by the spontaneous demonstrations of affection that met him wherever he went. He had taken the impressive pageantry of the Durbar in 1911 as proof that monarchy had a great role to play throughout the Empire; the unsophisticated diaries, in which he daily made brief notes on the weather, his engagements and on public affairs, show that, until his Jubilee in 1935, he had not fully realized how far the character of monarchical institutions had changed since he came to the throne.

The King had been shocked and indeed terrified by the tumbling of crowned heads during his reign; Sir Harold Nicolson calculates that in the twenty-five years he was on the throne five emperors, eight kings and eighteen minor dynasties came to an end. He was especially distressed by the assassination of his cousin, the Tsar, in 1917. When, inexperienced and untrained for his position, he came to the throne in 1910 he was immediately confronted with constitutional crises which looked like splitting the country and even plunging it into civil war. He survived these perils, and also lived through the alarming period of army discontent and revolutionary trade unionism that followed the war. He was also greatly relieved to discover that monarchy was in no way endangered by the two very loyal Labour Governments of 1924 and 1929, and he played a personal part in finding a Conservative solution for the constitutional and financial crisis of 1931. By 1935 it became manifest that the King was no longer a mere constitutional symbol but an object of personal veneration to a large part of the population. One of the main factors in bringing about this new and positive attitude to the Crown was the great success of the King as a broadcaster.

The high point of genuine royal popularity in England was attained by George V. People have now forgotten the public rejoicing during his Jubilee. London enjoyed a carnival only outdone in my experience on Armistice night 1918. For several days traffic in the busiest West End streets was stopped. The police were the centre of good-humoured rags. There was little drunkenness and an immense spontaneous demonstration of good humour. Those who are interested in anthropological parallels may amuse themselves by searching old newspapers for proof that the occasion was used as an emotional release, an orgy when the usually forbidden becomes permissible.[1]

At the death of George V we were finally able to gauge the strength of popular affection for him. When the old King died no one who talked to his neighbour on a bus, to the charwoman washing the steps or to a sightseer standing at the street corner, could doubt the almost universal feeling of loss, nor could any perceptive observer fail to notice the peculiarly personal character of this emotion. People who had never seen the King and only heard his voice on the wireless talked about him as if he were a personal friend or a near relative cut off in his prime. Propaganda, no doubt, accounts for much, but no propaganda can create this type of personal emotion unless the conditions are particularly favourable. Propaganda can exploit, spread, intensify existing emotion. It cannot create when the materials are lacking.

Here, I think, one can find the truth in a remark frequently heard at the death of George V. People constantly reiterated that King George was 'a father to us all'. He had become a universal father-figure. A process of identification of the royal family life with that of the individual life of the subject had begun during the previous half-century. This development dates from the last period of Queen Victoria. In his autobiography H. G. Wells describes how his mother followed everything in the life of the Queen with a passionate loyalty: she saw in the Queen a 'compensating personality', an ideal example of the sort of mother that she would have liked to have been. To such people the royal family provided a colour and a splendour which their own family lives too often lacked, but which they could none the less feel to be part of their own romance.

Adoration of the Crown could never have grown to such astonishing proportions had not the Monarchy during the last hundred years fitted so well the popular conception of what a

[1] A curious method of honouring the Jubilee was reported from Southport where, according to the *Evening Standard*, the magistrates decided that during the celebrations children over fourteen should be allowed to see films licensed for adults only.

monarch should be. In Queen Victoria people had learnt in the last decades of her reign to picture the perfect model of British motherhood. In Edward VII they saw a man who had outlived the follies of youth before he came to the throne (he had been publicly hissed as Prince of Wales) and had become, as they believed, the most genial type of sporting English gentleman. They believed, on no evidence at all, that he was a kind and good-tempered man (though, in fact, he was neither) and they imagined that he played a far greater part than any twentieth-century monarch could in cementing the *Entente* with France and in helping to preserve a peace that in fact was not preserved. But George V, as they constantly put it, was a 'good-living man', a model of what middle-class family man should be. The point has never been better put than by his son Edward in *A King's Story*:[f]

> 'It has always seemed to me that one of my father's great contributions to monarchical practice was the manner in which, without apparent design, he managed to resolve the internal contradiction of Monarchy in the twentieth century that requires it to be remote from, yet, at the same time, to personify the aspirations of, the people. It must appear aloof and distant in order to sustain the illusion of a Monarch who, shunning faction, stands above politics and the more mundane allegiances. At the same time, it must appear to share intimately the ideals of the multitude, whose affection and loyalty provide the broad base of constitutional Monarchy. My father, with the instinctive genius of the simple man, found the means of squaring the apparent circle within the resources of his own character. By the force of his own authentic example—the King himself in the rôle of the bearded paterfamilias, his devoted and queenly wife, their four grown sons and a daughter, not to mention the rising generation of grandchildren—he transformed the Crown as personified by the Royal Family into a model of the traditional family virtues, a model that was all the more genuine for its suspected but inconspicuous flaws. The King, as the dutiful father, became the living

symbol not only of the nation, but also of the Empire, the last link holding together these diversified and scattered communities.'

Edward VIII himself could never fulfil such an ideal conception. For many reasons, no doubt, but, above all, as he himself says, because he was a bachelor. Nevertheless he took up his royal burden 'in good heart', conscious that as Prince of Wales he was already an immensely popular figure throughout the Commonwealth. He had somewhat vaguely, but sincerely, a notion of being King in his own way, of giving the British concept of monarchy a new twentieth-century flavour.

Later in this book I shall consider in some detail the significance of the strange interlude of Edward VIII. His brother George, who had neither desired nor expected to be King, had many of the qualities that had made his father popular. His reign served to reinstate the pattern of monarchy, as George V had left it. It was only after Elizabeth's accession that the third period of royal public relations was inaugurated. This era may be properly called TV Monarchy. Some people hoped the accession of an attractive young Queen, with a handsome, well-educated and lively minded consort by her side, would mean an immediate relaxation of court protocol and the creation of a monarchical pattern more in tune with the mood of the British public after the Second World War. If Britain was to become a welfare state the logic would be a monarch of the Scandinavian type. In fact, the opportunity was used for very different ends. It was exploited by the half of Britain which preferred a windfall to a welfare state.

The reasons were twofold. The frozen hand of officialdom continued to dominate the palace and the concessions made to modernity and democratic sentiment were surprisingly meagre. Secondly, and far more important, the Establishment was in charge of the new channels of mass communication; like so many advertising agents, they seized on the potentialities of television to present the Queen and her relations in glorious technicolor. Whether they realized the dangers as well as the advantages of turning so garish a spotlight on all the members of the royal family is less certain. Photographers had long been careful to take pictures of royalty only in smiling mood. Television and the mass press has left little to the imagination.

In the following pages I have tried to deal faithfully with each of these periods. The story of British republicanism has never, to the best of my knowledge, been studied in any detail or given its proper place in the history of British thought. The backstage influence that the Crown exercised during the reign of Queen Victoria is well known, but comparatively few have realized that it continued in a particularly dangerous form during the First World War when George V was King. All this is history. What I have to say about the psychological and political effects of the new type of much-publicized monarchy necessarily involves controversial doctrine and personal speculation.

2

THE LIFE AND DEATH OF BRITISH
REPUBLICANISM

IT IS with something of a shock that we recall today what British newspapers said about monarchy a century ago. Take, as a prime example, the obituary tributes paid to George IV in 1830. The mourning bands round *The Times*, for instance, were as wide and black as they were when George V died a century later. But in 1830 black edging was not judged incompatible with a realistic description of the King's amours, an outspoken condemnation of his behaviour to his wife, who had found her place taken at court by a 'fashionable strumpet', or with the remark that 'the fact that he existed so long might, considering the habits of his earlier life, be looked upon as an extraordinary proof of the original vigour of his constitution'. On the day of his funeral the editorial comment in *The Times*, still in deep mourning, ran as follows:

'There never was an individual less regretted by his fellow-creatures than this deceased King. What eye has wept for him? What heart has heaved one sob of un-mercenary sorrow? . . . Has not his successor gained more upon the English tastes and prepossessions of his subjects by the blunt and unaffected—even should it be grotesque—cordiality of his demeanour, within a few short weeks than George IV—that Leviathan of *haut ton*—ever did during the sixty years of his existence? If George IV ever had a friend—a devoted friend in any rank of life—we protest that the name of him or her never reached us. An inveterate voluptuary, especially if he be an artificial person, is of all

27

known beings the most selfish. Selfishness is the true repel-
lant of human sympathy. Selfishness feels no attachment,
and invites none.

Nothing more remains to be done or said about George
IV, but to pay—as pay we must—for his profusion: and to
turn his bad conduct to some account by tying up the hands
of those who come after him in what concerns the public
money. At all events we shall always to the utmost of our
power do our duty—and we think we are unlikely to do it
flinchingly.'

The Times, which had always championed Queen Caroline
against the King, was particularly severe to George IV, but it
is also remarkable that it was ready to apply the adjective
'grotesque' to his successor. The word was apposite—Greville
tells us how, during the first ceremonials, William IV, pleasant
and jovial contrast as he was to his late brother, and capable
on occasion of presiding 'very decently' and looking like 'a
respectable old admiral', frequently caused so much embarrassment by his odd behaviour and extraordinary utterances that
ministers would beat a retreat, hide themselves or cover their
faces with their hands when he opened his mouth. His most
amiable utterances were sometimes disconcerting; in reply to
a deputation of freemasons who came to offer their loyal
obedience, William said: 'Gentlemen, if my love for you
equalled my ignorance of everything about you, it would be
boundless.'

Again *The Spectator*, which took the opposite side and
supported George IV against Queen Caroline, nevertheless
gave a list of his mistresses and said of His Majesty: 'A very
nice attention to the rigidities of moral observance can hardly
be asked from one who, to the vigour of youth and an eminently
handsome person, unites a complete command of fortune,
and whose will every man who surrounds him is more anxious
to flatter than to regulate. The King at a very early period of
his life gave evidence of his fondness for female society; a
failing of all others the most excusable, but it not infrequently
brings down on its possessor a degree of censure that the

William IV. 'A respectable old Admiral', by George Cruikshank

colder and darker vices of a disposition inherently evil do not provoke.' Of William IV the same paper wrote: 'On the throne, as in private life, William IV appears to have been a good-hearted man with frank impulses and kindly feelings; willing to do right but not infrequently doing wrong from want of knowledge and strength of mind. He had little information and

29

strong prejudices. Though sufficiently conceited and self-willed, he was easily imposed upon and led by the designing.' It added that: 'His late Majesty, though at times a jovial and, for a King, an honest man, was a weak, ignorant, commonplace sort of person. . . . Notwithstanding his feebleness of purpose and littleness of mind, his ignorance and his prejudices, William IV was to the last a popular sovereign, but his very popularity was acquired at the price of something like public contempt.'

The eighteen-thirties mark the nadir of English Monarchy. Republican and democratic sentiments—the two in those days seemed synonymous—which had swept through middle-class England after the French Revolution were re-emerging after the repression of the Napoleonic Wars at a moment when the royal family was politically and personally disreputable. The outburst of enthusiasm which made a heroine of Queen Caroline was due not so much to love of the Queen as to hatred of the King. And the public was right in detesting not merely George IV but all the sons of George III. The House of Commons would not so much have minded their sordid private lives if it had not been so frequently asked to pay their debts; it would even have tolerated that ogre the Duke of Cumberland if it had not known that he worked on George IV to resist Catholic emancipation, and it would merely have laughed at William IV if he had not thrown in his lot with the peers in obstructing the Reform Bill. To the followers of Paine and Godwin kings were the very symbol of tyranny and corruption. To overthrow the King seemed the first step in the recovery of the natural rights of man. Shelley spoke for insurgent England when he wrote: 'Oh, that the free would stamp the impious name of king into the dust.' And Thelwall epitomized a common sentiment when he blew the froth from his beer and said: 'So would I treat all kings.'

The more sober disciples of Bentham, who reached almost equally democratic conclusions by more laborious steps of argument, concluded that monarchy was an indefensible anomaly. If the greatest happiness of the greatest number was the criterion of government, then a majority decision must always be better than a minority one. All secret influences, all minorities in privileged positions, were 'sinister', and the least defensible and most sinister of all was the influence of a single man wielding a final veto and an incalculable influence over political decisions.

If the King exercised power he interfered with the automatic perfection of democratic machinery; if, on the other hand, he was obedient to his democratically elected ministers, why pay him for doing nothing? According to the mathematical reasoning of Bentham and James Mill it was demonstrable that monarchy was the worst possible form of government; majority government meant that the will and, therefore, the happiness of the majority would be obeyed; in an oligarchy only the pleasures of the minority would be served; in a monarchy, by definition, the general happiness would defer to the wishes or influence of one man and his immediate entourage. It is to be noticed that when Macaulay unmercifully ridiculed James Mill's mathematical demonstration of the advantages of democracy, he attacked his method of reasoning and not his conclusions. He was content to point out that if the thesis of democracy were pushed too far the rule of the middle class might not be as safe as Mill assumed, since, in the long run, the interests of the majority were antagonistic to the privileges of property. It was not until 1866 that Bagehot took the first step towards modern theory and introduced psychological arguments. He argued that we paid the Crown not to exercise specific functions but to retain the loyalty of 'the labourer in Somerset', who could not understand the process of government but who could respond to the drama of royalty and feel a primitive and sentimental loyalty for the personality of the Queen.

It is often, but wrongly, assumed that attacks on the Crown ended with the disappearance of the disreputable sons of George III. In fact republicanism remained part of the accepted creed of the radical middle and working classes until the 'seventies. The Reform Bill of 1832 was regarded merely as the beginning of a revolution which would lead not only to universal suffrage but also to the dis-establishment of the Church and abolition of all hereditary institutions, including the House of Lords and the Monarchy. The Chartist Movement, already well under way when the Queen came to the throne, did not include the abolition of the Monarchy in the six points of the Charter only because it assumed that monarchy, like other medieval relics, would disappear when the working class attained political power.

Many short-lived working-class papers struggled to exist in the mid-nineteenth century. Some were outspokenly republican; others, only by implication. Among those who did not hesitate to speak their minds was W. J. Linton, famous in his day as a working-class poet and fine wood-engraver. He wrote republican poems against the Monarchy from his rural retreat in Westmorland.[a] His paper, the *English Republic*, which carried his own engravings, lasted from 1851 to 1855. But Linton was a lone figure with an almost mystical approach, compounded of Rousseau and primitive Christianity. George Julian Harney, the Chartist leader, had nothing mystical about him.[b] He served several gaol sentences for aiding Hetherington, who published his *Poor Man's Guardian* in defiance of the 'taxes on knowledge'. Harney met Karl Marx when he and Engels were in London in 1847 at the Communist Congress which commissioned them to write *The Communist Manifesto*. Harney had worked with Feargus O'Connor on the *Northern Star*, but parted from him when he was not allowed to advocate a socialist republic. His *Democratic Review* treated revolution as inevitable; monarchy would disappear with landlordism and the Empire. The French, German and Hungarian revolutions of 1848 everywhere inspired hopes of republican success; America had blazed the trail; Australia was 'democratic at heart' and Ireland would fight for its freedom as a republic. The triumph of reaction in 1849 confirmed Harney's view that revolution could not succeed without force. In October 1849 he wrote: 'I do not believe that the people of Paris have finally renounced powder and lead. . . . I have no faith that the people will conquer "the promised land" by the force of mere ideas.'

Harney and his friends were not mealy-mouthed. Republicans had called William IV 'Mr. Guelph' and the Queen was 'Madame Guelph'. They were after all not more rude than those who shouted 'Mrs. Melbourne' after her when she appeared with Sir Robert Peel during her struggle over 'the bedchamber question'.[1]

Nothing so much accounted for the immense popularity of that persistent Whig, Lord Palmerston, as his often quite undiplomatic support for Continental rebels. As Foreign Secretary, he was quite ready to encourage criticism of the Crown, and allowed it to be known that the Queen and Albert objected to the friendly reception he was prepared to give to Kossuth and other refugees from European monarchs who

---

[1] Cf. also the following from *Punch*, 6 November 1841, during the pregnancy of the Queen. The future Edward VII was born on 9 November.

'THE LORD MAYORS AND THE QUEEN

The interesting condition of Her Majesty is a source of the most agonising suspense to the Lord Mayors of London and Dublin, who, if a Prince of Wales is not born before their office expires, will lose the chance of being created baronets.

According to rumour, the baby—we beg pardon, the scion of the House of Brunswick, was to have been born—we must apologise again, we should say was to have been added to the illustrious stock of the reigning family of Great Britain—some day last month, and, of course, the present Lord Mayors had comfortably made up their minds that they should be entitled to the dignity it is customary to confer on such occasions as that which the nation now ardently anticipates. But here we are at the beginning of November and no Prince of Wales. We have reason to know that the Lord Mayor of London has not slept a wink since Saturday, and his Lady has not smiled, according to an authority on which we are accustomed to rely, since Thursday fortnight. Some say it is done on purpose, because the present official is Tory; and others insinuate that the Prince of Wales is postponed on order that there may be an opportunity of making Daniel O'Connell a baronet. Others suggest that there will be twins presented to the nation, one on the night of November 8, the other on the morning of the 9th, so as to conciliate both parties, but we are not at present disposed to pronounce a decided opinion on this part of the question. We know that politics have been carried most indelicately into the very heart of the Royal household. But we hope, for the honour of all parties, that the confinement of the Queen is not made a matter of political arrangement.'

Christening of H.R.H. the Prince of Wales, A.D. 1841

The Royal Cot

Usher of the
Black Rod

The Dry Nurses

Pap Bearers to
H.R.H. the Prince
of Wales

Napkin bearers
to ditto

The Wet Nurses

Knights of the Garter

The Sword of State
borne by the Duke
of Wellington

The Arch-Bishop of
Canterbury, with the
Baptism Water out
of the Jordan

Bishops

Her most Gracious Majesty the Queen
and Her Illustrious Consort Prince Albert

Tail Bearers

were friends and relatives of the Queen. When Palmerston was summarily dismissed in 1851, because of his incorrigible habit of sending foreign dispatches abroad without giving the Queen and Prince Albert the opportunity of objecting to them, he declared himself a victim of foreign intrigue; and the chief impact of the incident, which the pundits of the moment thought had ended his career, was to reinforce his popularity as a sporting champion of Liberalism and to put into people's heads the idea that the British Court was conspiring with Continental courts to frustrate the wishes of British democracy. Thus, when he resigned on the eve of the Crimean War, it was almost universally believed that he had been again dismissed by the Crown. So violent was the newspaper outcry that the Queen, outraged by daily accusations that her husband was a traitor in league with foreign governments, wrote long letters to the Prime Minister, threatening, in words even more undisciplined and heavily underlined than usual, to abdicate the throne and abandon her ungrateful people.

On 4 January she wrote to the Premier:

'The Queen had hoped that the scandalous attacks which had appeared immediately after the resignation of Lord Palmerston against the Prince in several (though none of the *most* respectable) papers would cease, and, indeed, *had* done so, but she has been mistaken; she perceives that a *systematic* and *most infamous* attack appears daily in *The Morning Herald* and *Standard*, and she, therefore, can no longer *doubt* that there is some design in *this*, which, as Lord Aberdeen will easily believe, she DEEPLY *resents*.'

She felt that the more serious charges should be met: Albert should be given a constitutional position.

'Therefore, upon mature reflection, and after considering the question for nearly eleven years, I have come to the conclusion (and I know the Prince has also) that the *Title* which is now by *universal consent* given him of "*Prince Consort*" *with the highest rank in and out of Parliament*, IMMEDIATELY after the Queen, and before EVERY OTHER PRINCE of the Royal Family, should be the one assigned to the HUSBAND of the QUEEN REGNANT *once and for all*.'

Lord Aberdeen was sympathetic and believed that the attack would die down. *The Times*, at any rate, represented serious opinion and would take no part in the agitation. But Delane was not sufficiently cautious. In defending Prince Albert he admitted difficulties in the Prince Consort's constitutional position.

This wrung another letter from the Queen, who complained that the Government had allowed even *The Times* to print a 'very injudicious article'. 'If the country,' she proceeded, '*really has* such incomprehensible and reprehensible notions, there is no remedy but the introduction of the *Salic Law*, for which she would *heartily* vote. A *woman must have* a support and an adviser; and *who can* this *properly* be but her husband, *whose duty it is to watch over her interests private and public.* From this *sacred* duty NO EARTHLY POWER can absolve him! Were it not for the Prince, the Queen's health and strength would long since have sunk under the multifarious duties of her position as Queen and the mother of a large family. Were the Queen to *believe* that these unprincipled and immoral insinuations really were those of *any* but a wicked and despicable few, she would LEAVE a position which nothing but her domestic happiness could make her endure and retire to private life— leaving the country to choose another ruler after their own HEART'S CONTENT. But she does *not* think so ill of her country, though she may say that these disgraceful exhibitions will leave behind them *very bitter* feelings in her breast, which time alone can eradicate!

'If the whole *is* brought before Parliament, which would be better but which seems almost doubtful now, the Queen hopes it will be on the first *night* of the Session, and done with.

'The Queen encloses an extract from her journal of the year 1841 giving *Lord Melbourne's* opinion of the Prince and his position; the Prince was only twenty-two then!'ᶜ

In a parliamentary debate that followed the Queen declared herself satisfied by the Minister's defence of Albert. In truth on the particular issue which led to the attack on him the Prince was right and the public was wrong. But the public was justified in fearing the close contact between the British throne and the reactionary heads of Continental governments. If more had been known of the influence of Baron Stockmar, Albert's mentor, who held strong views about the powers that he thought still belonged to the British Crown, or about the Queen's highly confidential correspondence with her uncle, the King of the Belgians, the attack would have been even more widespread and threatening.

The Prince was an easy target for the press of the period. Albert was unpopular with all classes. The public regarded him merely as another German who had wormed his way into British political life. Memories of George III's sons were not dead. Albert was also disliked by the aristocracy. Not only was he 'unEnglish', but he showed it by being an indifferent horseman; a chess player, not a race-goer; he was unfashionable, unco guid, and given to philanthropy, the study of social statistics, science and philosophy. He thought that the condition of the people in question—especially their appalling housing— deserved the attention of ministers and even of royalty; he tried in vain to convince politicians that there was something wrong with the education of England when 'out of 4,908,696 children only some 2,861,848 had any instruction at all and more than half of these went to school for only two years'. The Great Exhibition of 1851 was only one of the many enlightened activities he patronized or originated in the vain hope of making English people interested in science, music, learning or the arts.

Such off-beat interests were no road to popularity in mid-nineteenth-century Britain and the press found it easy to attack a German prince in language it could scarcely have used about the Queen herself. Today we may hold that Albert was justified in trying to prevent one of the most unnecessary and ill-prepared wars in British history; if he had succeeded in obtaining a settlement with the Tsar in 1854 he would have been entitled to the same praise that historians have awarded him for his part in preventing war with the United States seven years later. In 1854, however, the populace saw the situation in simple and dramatic form as a battle between the reactionary forces led by the infamous Tsar and supported by the Prince Consort, and Liberalism championed by Palmerston and strangely personified in the Sultan of Turkey. The papers, some of which, in the early stages of the attack, were directly inspired by Palmerston himself, talked of 'treachery in high places', of the 'hidden power' and of 'a certain illustrious personage' who had 'a third key to the dispatch box'. They said that he thought 'none but Germans have the right or title to interfere in the government of this country', and traced his foreign connection and accused him of being a tool of the Tsar. It was popularly believed that he was imprisoned in the Tower as a traitor.

Albert's patriotism during the war won him public respect, if never affection. We must remember, wild though the attack was, that it was not without some constitutional justification. Had the Prince any legal right to take part in the government of England? At the time of her marriage the Queen sought to obtain the assent of her ministers to accord Albert a constitutional status equal to her own; she even toyed with the idea of making him King and she failed to win for him the title of Prince Consort. The best she could do in 1841 was, by her own prerogative, to issue Letters Patent declaring that Albert should be styled His Royal Highness with the right to 'have, hold and enjoy pre-eminence and precedence next to herself'. Sixteen years later, again by the Queen's prerogative, he was given the title of Prince Consort; until then, she complained, difficulties were caused when she and her husband went abroad by the pettiness of foreign royalties who refused to recognize Albert as anything more than the 'younger brother of the Duke of Saxe-Coburg and Gotha'. Albert's own modest view of himself was that he was 'the Queen's private secretary and permanent Minister'—a position that by the nature of things could not be denied him.

In 1854 nothing had been done to convince the British people that Albert thought or felt as an Englishman. The *Daily News*, in an article that caused peculiar offence to Albert and the Queen, spoke for a large section of British opinion when, after paying tribute to the Prince's personal qualities, it said:

'We never expected that, educated as he has been, connected as he is by family ties, he could ever be brought to feel and act as an English Liberal!'[1]

The vehement radicalism, which had been stirred by the revolutions of 1848 and turned into passionate indignation against all tyrants and despots during the reaction of 1849, exhausted itself in the ghastly futility of the Crimean War. But it remained the dominant creed of the working class and of the petty bourgeoisie in the 'sixties. It was kept alive in the struggle for Italian independence by popular hatred of tyrants like Bomba, when Gladstone protested against the horrors of Neapolitan prisons, and by the visits to England of national revolutionaries like Mazzini, Kossuth and Garibaldi. Sometimes it was the Tsar who appeared as the personification of reactionary tyranny, sometimes the Emperor, Napoleon III. When Simon Bernard was tried for complicity in Orsini's attempt to murder the French Emperor he was triumphantly acquitted by a Middlesex jury though all the evidence pointed to his guilt. Every democratic movement on the Continent was enthusiastically welcomed. *The Times*, under Delane's editorship, was almost as fierce in denouncing despots as the cheaper and less respectable press. When Garibaldi came to England in 1864 he was received as if he were a British and not an Italian national hero, and was hurried out of the country for fear of international fuss.

In 1861 Albert the Good died. In the last years of his life he had become King of England in all but name. It may be doubted whether England ever had a more conscientious, hardworking or better-informed king. He was a crashing bore, no doubt, and a peculiarly Teutonic kind of bore. His advice, however, was serious and influential and he embarrassed ministers by knowing more about foreign affairs than they did. Intellectually and emotionally he dominated the Queen. For years after his death she was distraught and for months was

---

[1] Theodore Martin, *Life of the Prince Consort*, Vol. II, p. 541. The *Daily News* went on: 'to speak of the prince as one who has breathed from childhood the air of Courts tainted by the imaginative servility of Goethe —who has been indoctrinated in early manhood in the stationary or retrograde political principles of the school of Niebuhr and Savigny'.

Punch: 22 December 1855

More Noble Conduct of H.R.H.F.M.P.A. He wishes to be placed on the same Footing as his more Fortunate Brethren in the Line!

unable to attend to public business. She found relief in drama-
tizing her grief and deifying Albert's memory. The story has
often been told of how, until her death, everything in his
apartments was kept precisely as it was when he died; even
his dress suit was laid out on his bed every night during the
forty years that the Queen survived him. As time went on,
she formed an extraordinary attachment to Albert's favourite
gillie, John Brown. She brought him with her to Osborne and
Windsor and in effect permitted him to control her household.
Boorish, arrogant, hard-drinking and utterly disrespectful, his
conduct infuriated the royal family and indeed all who had to
be in touch with the Queen. In the Highlands her habit was to
go out alone with him for the day provided only with sand-
wiches and whisky. She would listen to no protest from the
Prince of Wales or other exalted personages who dared to
complain that Brown spoke to them as if he were king and
they were his servants. So assured was Brown's possessiveness
and familiarity towards the Queen that scandal was inevitable.
It has been seriously argued that the rumours about their
relationship which were rife at the time may have had some
basis in fact. A recent book suggests that they may in fact have
been lovers.[d] It will need far more than the flimsy evidence
produced by Mr. Tisdall to make the public believe a story so
fundamentally contrary to the accepted image of Queen
Victoria. All that is relevant here is that a pamphlet entitled
Mrs. John Brown seems to have been privately printed and
circulated and that it alleged that the Queen was secretly
married to Brown. The Queen was also said to have had a
child by him. When told about the pamphlet in old age the
Queen laughed, saying she had no idea that she had ever been
so notorious a person. What is certain is that ribald jesters
called her 'Mrs. Brown', that rude cartoons about the Queen
and John Brown appeared in a publication called the *Tomahawk*,
and that her seclusion greatly encouraged republican sentiment.
The polite way of attacking the Monarchy at this period,
however, was to point to the fact that in seclusion the Queen
annually received, and hoarded, a large sum of public money
and performed no corresponding function. People who listened

to no scandal read with agreement the widely circulated pamphlet called *What does she do with it?*

A further impulse was given to the radical republicanism of the 'sixties by the success of the North in the American Civil War. British opinion was sharply divided. The upper classes were broadly in favour of a Southern victory; the North stood in the minds of British radicals as the symbol of the new, free, republican world which offered a pattern of government to which every nation must in time conform. In April 1865 Professor Beesly, writing in *The Beehive*,ᵉ a pioneering Trade Union paper, celebrated the victory of the North by saying that 'the time has come when those who have unswervingly supported the Republican cause . . . at length find themselves in possession of the field, their opinions vindicated . . . and their opponents silenced and abashed'. With a touch of prophetic insight, matched by a pardonable over-optimism, he concluded that the diehard critics of republicanism, who had supported the South in the hope that its victory would destroy the 'great Republic', 'may rely upon it that a vast impetus has been given to Republican sentiment in England and that they will have to reckon with it before long'.

The fall of Napoleon and the proclamation of the Third Republic on 4 September 1870 seemed finally to clinch the matter. Radicals of the middle class assumed a republican future. Men like Charles Dilke, John Morley and Frederick Harrison, Oxford intellectuals, had associated themselves with French intellectuals who led the struggle against dictatorship on the Continent. If a republic was declared in France why not in England? Swinburne, the *avant-garde* poet of the time, heralded a new age with an *Ode on the Proclamation of the French Republic* and he challenged the Establishment with *Songs Before Sunrise*. The moment seemed ripe; the Queen in retirement was an expensive affront to commonsense, and the private life of the Prince of Wales, after the Mordaunt divorce case, had become a subject of public gossip.

Working-class revolutionaries, in the doldrums since the

defeat of Chartism, quickly responded to the news of republican-ism across the Channel. *The Times* estimated that 5,000 people rallied to the first of a series of mass demonstrations in Hyde Park. At this meeting on 18 September George Odger, the chief speaker, was dispatched to Paris to make contact with Jules Favre, the republican Foreign Secretary. At the next mass rally in Trafalgar Square *Reynolds* talked of a crowd of 20,000 and at a further meeting in Hyde Park of 50,000; and *The Times* reported that the crowd was 'overwhelmingly large'. Mass meetings were held throughout the country during the whole of the next twelve months. The authorities were only partially successful in banning such meetings to army volun-teers; in some areas they tried to stop them being held. At a Trafalgar Square demonstration on 18 December 1870 con-tingents with brass bands arrived from Clerkenwell, Mile End, Hackney and Deptford; speeches were made by Bradlaugh and a French journalist on the staff of *La Liberté*, who arrived by balloon. On 24 January one of the first republican clubs was founded in Birmingham; London followed in April, and in the course of the year similar republican clubs sprouted in almost every large town in England.[f] Excitement increased during the months of the Paris Commune (18 March to 28 May). *The Times* said that a Hyde Park demonstration on 16 April was attended by 'roughs, domestic servants and trading classes', but added that the leaders attacked one another and showed no 'community of feeling'. On 7 May a Universal Republican League was formed—an abortive 'national' movement which, like so many working-class organizations, petered out. The apostles of 'revolution through physical force' quarrelled, ideo-logically rather than practically, with those who advocated 'moral suasion'. Their influence was weakened by reports of violence and atrocities in France. The upshot was usually the dispatch of a deputation to sympathetic M.P.s.

Nor were sympathetic M.Ps. lacking. Side by side with these mass demonstrations were smaller London gatherings, held in St. James's Hall or the New Hall of Science. The initiative came from positivists like Professor Beesly, who were quickly joined by the then radicals and secularists like Holyoake, Sir

Henry Hoare (joint M.P. for Chelsea with Sir Charles Dilke) and, above all, Charles Bradlaugh.[g]

In January 1871 Sir Charles Dilke, P. A. Taylor (M.P. for Leicester) and Professor Fawcett (M.P. for Brighton) vehemently opposed a House of Commons vote for a dowry and annuity for the Princess Louise. In July something like a sustained campaign was maintained in the press and in meetings and demonstrations against another proposal to grant an annuity of £30,000—this time for Prince Arthur. The issue was debated in the House in July; fifty M.P.s supported Mr. Dixon's amendment to reduce the figure by £10,000, and eleven M.P.s were bold enough to vote against any annuity at all.

Mr. Dixon said that 'it was not to be denied that a republican feeling had sprung up and was increasing rapidly among the working classes of this country'.[h] This was, at the moment, difficult to deny. Even while he was speaking a demonstration against the annuity was in full blast in Trafalgar Square. It took place in spite of a police ban on all meetings in the square. *The Times* said that 'it proved to be one of the largest gatherings ever known in the chosen scene of demonstrations'.

The peak of British republicanism was probably reached in November 1871 when Sir Charles Dilke and other Liberal politicians felt sufficiently encouraged by popular feeling to come openly into the arena in favour of a republic. A large part of the British middle class was nonconformist in religion and utilitarian in philosophy. They were shocked at Bradlaugh's atheism and horrified by his advocacy of birth control, but, provided the point was stated by a more respectable orator, they were ready to agree with the argument advanced in his widely circulated pamphlet *An Impeachment of the House of Brunswick*. Why, he demanded, should they be taxed to pay for a rich Queen who performed no public services? He added that in a few years Britain would be ready for a republic and that it was his 'earnest desire that the present Prince of Wales should never dishonour this country by becoming King'.

The view that a republic was not far off was encouraged by a slip in a speech by Disraeli. Eloquently defending the Queen in her retirement, he explained that she was 'physically and

morally incapacitated from performing her duties'. The phrase
was grist to the mill of republicans and Disraeli had to explain
himself to the Queen. He wrote to Sir William Jenner, her
physician: 'I need not assure you that the epithet *moral*
involves *mental* no more than the epithet *physical* does. What I
meant to convey was that neither Her Majesty's frame nor
feelings could at present bear the strain and burthen of the
pageantry of State. After I had used the word it was suggested
to me that it might be misinterpreted by the simple, and I
requested the reporters to omit it. I understood they willingly
agreed to do so; but it seems the *Daily Telegraph* could not
resist the opportunity of attempting a sensation.[i]

Sir Charles Dilke opened his campaign in November 1871
with a meeting at the radical stronghold of Newcastle. Others
followed at Reading, Leeds and Bolton. According to *Reynolds*
the Tories were responsible for 'fearful riots' at these meetings.
At Bolton bricks were thrown through the windows and one
republican supporter was killed. At the very large meeting at
Leeds Dilke declared that his main object was to defend the
right to speak freely, even about the Crown. On 6 December
a meeting was held in Birmingham Town Hall with Joseph
Chamberlain as Mayor presiding; several hundred interrupters
were turned out by the police.

Dilke's argument was that England was already to all
intents and purposes a republic. 'Have we not republican
virtues and republican spirit?' he asked at Newcastle. 'Have we
not the fact of self-government? Are we not gaining general
education? Well, if you can show me a fair chance that a
republic here would be free from political corruption that
hangs about the Monarchy, I say, for my part—and I believe
the middle class in general would say—let it come.' He argued
that the Queen was guilty of 'a diversion of public monies
almost amounting to malversation'. Here, as he afterwards
admitted, he made a mistake. Referring to the Queen's
enormous wealth and the large income which the State gave
her, although she no longer performed even ceremonial
functions, Sir Charles asserted that she paid no income tax—a
statement which gave Mr. Gladstone an effective debating

Punch: 23 September 1865

Queen Hermione. Paulina (Britannia) unveils the statue.
'Tis time! Descend; be stone no more!'—*Winter's Tale, Act V,*
Scene 3

answer when the matter was discussed in the House of Commons a few months later.

Sir Charles's speech was severely criticized in the press. If the Crown, said *The Times*, were again to show a disposition to meddlesome obstructiveness like that of George III, or if the private life of the monarch resembled that of George IV, the establishment of a republic would be a contingency to be faced. In the absence of such a contingency (which God forbid should ever arise) 'it was recklessness bordering on criminality' to raise the question. Sir Charles Dilke must either openly declare for a republic (which he did not do) or refrain from vilifying the Monarchy. It was, of course, possible that a republic might come, and it was regrettable that the Queen was so often in retirement at Balmoral or Osborne when she was most needed in or near London. Of course, she made every effort to discharge her duties. But 'we have pointed out before and we point out again that no feeling of loyalty, however fervent, can be proof for ever against such a strain'. If Dilke wanted to raise the question of the Civil List he was entitled to do so in the House of Commons; it was wicked to do so before an audience of working men.

Dilke was by no means abashed, while colleagues in the campaign wrote and congratulated him. Joseph Chamberlain wrote: 'The Republic must come, and at the rate at which we are moving it will come in our generation. The greater is the necessity for discussing its conditions beforehand and for a clear recognition of what we may lose as well as what we should gain.'

John Morley, who had become editor of the *Fortnightly Review*—and in those days the political thinking of England was done in such periodicals—asked Frederick Harrison for a long article setting forth the argument for a British republic. His article stands as the peak of British republican thought in the nineteenth century. He rebuked Disraeli for trying to elevate the throne and for introducing 'intentional unction into the accepted language of homage'. In a sentence which reads ironically enough today, when we know the part that Queen Victoria really played in government, Harrison wrote

The Baccarat Case, June 1891. Sir W. Gordon-Cumming in the witness box and Edward, Prince of Wales, seated in front of him.

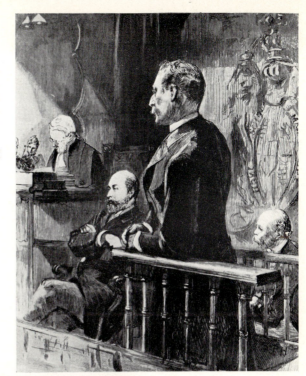

As Others See Us. Queen Victoria nurses the future Edward VIII: Edward VII (then Prince of Wales) and George V (then Duke of York) stand behind her.

Highland Jinks: Edward VII

Four Monarchs of the Glen: George V, Edward VII, Edward VIII and George VI

that 'the sovereign is as much bound to keep his feelings to himself as any well-bred young lady. In consequence the influence of the throne, whatever it may be socially, is nothing politically. . . .' Disraeli was attempting 'to inscribe "the Throne" as a new watchword on the banner of his party . . . the formation of a genuine Beefeater-party, whose political mission is to rally round the throne, is certainly a new feature in Party history'. The republican's task was 'to lift the subject from the cataract of cant in which it had been drowned. In the truest sense of the word, this country is and had long been a Republic, though an imperfect Republic it must be allowed. . . . England is now an aristocractic Republic, with a democratic machinery and an hereditary grandmaster of the ceremonies. For a Republic is that State the principle of which is not privilege but merit, where all public power is a free gift and is freely entrusted to those who seem able to use it best.' Monarchy in England had merely become a survival, an 'otiose tail', a rudimentary organ atrophied for want of use. 'The most silent member of Parliament has more legislative power than the Crown.' The Crown had some appearance of power at a change of ministry, but the actual control was in the hands of the out-going Prime Minister. 'In extreme case a venerable peer—a sort of family lawyer—is confidentially called in.' If the Crown were 'to insist on personally nominating a minister the House of Commons would sharply call him to order . . . the very lawn of the bishops would ruffle in wrath. We may, however, be perfectly tranquil. No sovereign is likely to attempt any gambols with the constitution, any more than the cream-coloured horses are likely to kick to pieces the ginger-bread coach.'

By the time these words appeared in print the little wave of republicanism had fallen back into the eternal ocean of sentimentality. The effect of Dilke's campaign was more than counteracted by the long and dangerous illness of the Prince of Wales at the end of 1871. The picture of the Queen, watching at the bedside of her son, evoked widespread sympathy and there was a general rally in the press to the side of the throne. The more extreme radical papers were not, it is true, much

affected. *Reynolds*, which combined sex, police-court scandal
and radical politics for the working classes, seized the opportunity to denounce 'the mean, toadying, craven spirit of so-
called loyalty'. It objected especially to the 'great epidemic of
typhoid loyalty': the Prince was supposed to have caught
infection from the drains; ordinary people died daily from such
infection and no one noticed it. They hoped that if the Prince
recovered he would spend the ability that he had so far shown
at Hurlingham in getting a pure water supply for the people.
So far, 'he has been weighed in the balance by the large
majority of the people and found sadly wanting'. They hoped
that Dilke, like Latimer, had 'by God's grace, lighted a candle
in England which would never be put out'.

The republican issue was debated in March 1872, when
Dilke defended his attack on the Civil List. His idea was, he
said, to make his speech 'solid and full of matter but studiously
dull'. He was seconded by Auberon Herbert, a charming and
unusual figure in politics, an aristocrat, philosopher and artist.
His speech caused something like a riot in the House. In the
midst of the turmoil three attempts were made to count out the
motion. Strangers were spied and the galleries cleared. Henry
Fawcett, who had founded a republican club in Cambridge,
refused to support Dilke, because he was determined 'in the
most emphatic way possible to protest against the question of
republicanism being raised upon a miserable haggle over a few
pounds'. Gladstone replied with vehemence and sarcasm, paid
compliments to the Queen, denied Dilke's allegations about
income tax and asked whether it was decent 'to reopen a life-
bargain with the sovereign'.

This was not the end of British republicanism, though in
its later stages it made an odd alliance with 'Henry Georgism'.
In 1873 a republican conference at Birmingham entrusted
Bradlaugh with a message of congratulation to the new
republican government in Spain. A substantial parliamentary
group continued to protest at successive grants of public
money to members of the royal family as they arrived at their

Punch: 15 April 1878

'New Crowns for Old Ones!' (Aladdin *adapted*). The Bill for adding to the Royal Titles that of Empress of India, though pressed forward by the Government, was scarcely approved by the country—1876

majority or married.ʲ The annual Budget at this time was about seventy million a year and the cost of the royal family about one million. Some royal expenses were not included in the Civil List and appeared under other items in the estimates. Even during this period of acute economic depression, radical criticism was not socialist; it was merely a logical deduction from the principles of Gladstonian finance. Its cogency lay in the fact that anyone who cared to look could see that many people in Britain were actually starving. The more courageous radicals hoped to reduce misery by cutting a large item of unnecessary public expenditure.

Economy was the main argument. But these intermittent attacks on royal subsidies had another aspect. They were one expression of a rearguard action against the new imperialism. Radicals watched with dismay while Disraeli built up the imperial idea and associated it with the Queen. They did not know, of course, how far Disraeli's flattery went; they could not guess that the Queen was told that she was the real ruler of England, and they had no conception to what length of interference, and indeed of unconstitutionality, she was prepared to go when a Liberal ministry, which she hated, was substituted for the government of her beloved Lord Beaconsfield. But they protested, and carried some Tories with them, when, on the Queen's own initiative, he promoted the Royal Titles Bill, which made her Empress of India. They did what they could by rallying behind Gladstone to check Disraeli's autocratic conduct of foreign policy. Parliament was studiously neglected, while Beaconsfield, acting on behalf of the Queen, made a treaty with Russia, summoned Indian troops to Malta, and bought the shares that gave Britain control of the Suez Canal. Discontent was apparent in the unfavourable reception given to Volume III of Theodore Martin's *Life of the Prince Consort*, which was generally interpreted as a message from the Crown to the nation.

In 1879 the House of Commons actually debated the dangerous growth of the power of the Crown. On the economic side, the demand for the reduction of the Civil List continued until 1885, when Bradlaugh took his seat and reinforced the republican group in the House. Gladstone, who could have revived republicanism by telling a tithe of what he suffered from the Queen, was a devout royalist and an unusually scrupulous politician. He held his tongue, and Disraeli's brilliant manœuvre, when he brought the Queen from her retirement, and in a single speech identified imperialism with Conservatism, and associated them both with loyalty to the Monarchy, was allowed to succeed. Only a few years before Beaconsfield had himself spoken of the 'wretched colonies' as a 'millstone round our necks'. He had thus accepted the current view of Conservative as well as Liberal politicians and permanent officials of the Colonial Office, that as colonies grew up they would necessarily break with the mother-country. It was Disraeli's peculiar genius to see in 1872 that the new imperialist movement which had been growing in the 'sixties in the minds of federalists like Froude, Sir George Grey and W. E. Forster might be made into an asset for the Conservative Party.

We must not, of course, attribute too much to Disraeli. Republicanism would have failed and the new imperialism won in any case. Many things conspired to check the growth of the republican creed. The climate of Europe changed in the seventies; French democratic ideas were overshadowed by the blood and iron of Bismark. At Oxford the modified Hegelianism of T. H. Green took the place of the utilitarianism of Mill, while socialism won its way as the working-class creed in the place of the old-fashioned radicalism. We may detect deep economic causes behind these developments; it is easy to see why British manufacturers and merchants, whose virtual monopoly of the raw materials and markets of the world was now challenged by the competition of Germany, America and Japan, were likely to turn to a creed that made for the consolidation and extension of the British Empire. Economic historians choose 1870 as a convenient date to mark the second industrial revolution. With the home market satiated, British capitalism turned to undeveloped Africa.

Politically we see the change epitomized in the transference of the middle-class vote of Birmingham from the pacifist, free trade, Little Englandism of Bright to the protectionist imperialism of Joseph Chamberlain. There were strong forces at work; the last anti-imperialistic government of England, Gladstone's second ministry, failed, not because of the Irish rumpus in the House, or of the affair of Bradlaugh's exclusion from Parliament, but because Liberalism had no policy with which to meet the new Empire problems which arose in South Africa and the Sudan. And when Liberalism was again returned with a triumphant majority, twenty years later, it was led by men who had learnt the new imperialistic philosophy at Oxford. Their ideas were as remote from those of Gladstone or Mill as from the republicanism which had seemed to the young Dilke and Chamberlain to be the inevitable creed of the future.

Yet Disraeli's part in 1872 was important. The effect of his Crystal Palace speech was to blend into one imperial emotion the problem of the white dominions, the problem of Ireland, the problem of the Near East, the problem of India, and finally, by a stroke of genius, the problem of the Queen's relationship to her subjects. Henceforward it was impossible to induce anyone to think clearly and coolly about any of these issues. It became impossible to hint at the necessity of Home Rule in Ireland or to demand better government in India, or to discuss the ethics of British occupation in Egypt, without being charged with disloyalty to the Queen. To turn an intelligent imperialist movement into a popular jingoism, which bore fruit in the Boer War, was the immediate result of Disraeli's exploitation of the Crown. Propaganda for the Empire and for the Monarchy went hand in hand. The Crown had become a symbol of national greatness. Very few people had any idea that it was more than a symbol. They did not know that it also exercised a powerful influence on the government of Britain.

In the twentieth century republicanism has never been a serious issue of British politics. Most socialists would say that they are opposed to all hereditary privileges in politics and the Labour Party has repeatedly voted for the abolition of the

House of Lords. But Labour has never gone on record as demanding, even theoretically, the end of the Monarchy. Perhaps the clue to the attitude of the politically conscious working class is best found in Keir Hardie, who regarded the Crown as part of an aristocratic racket, but who thought the real issue was socialism. In 1897, at the time of Queen Victoria's Diamond Jubilee, he wrote:

'The cheering millions would be there and cheer just as lustily if the occasion were the installation of the first President of the British Republic; the soldiers are there because they are paid for coming, and nine out of every ten of them will heartily curse the whole affair as a disagreeable and irksome additional duty; the statesmen are there because Empire means trade and trade means profit. Even under a representative system of government it is possible to paralyse a nation by maintaining the fiction that a reigning family is a necessity of good government.'

But even Hardie thought it not worth while to advocate a republic.

'In this country loyalty to Queen is used by the profitmongers to blind the eyes of the people; in America loyalty to the flag serves the same purpose. Law and order, by which the commoners are kept quiet whilst they are being fleeced by their masters, must have a symbol and anything will serve. Therefore, until the system of wealth production be changed, it is not worth exchanging a queen for a president. The robbery of the poor would go on equally under the one as the other. The king fraud will disappear when the exploiting of the people draws to a close.'k

Still a Member of Parliament when the future Edward VIII was born, Keir Hardie complained about the fuss made over a royal baby. He remarked, in what the Duke of Windsor himself describes as 'an uncannily clairvoyant' prophecy, that there was no way of knowing whether the future king would have 'qualifications of fitness for the position'. He would always 'be surrounded by sycophants and flatterers' and taught that he was a superior being. 'In due course, following the precedent which has already been set, he will be sent on a tour round the world, and probably rumours of a morganatic marriage will follow, and the end of it will be that the country will be called upon to pay the bill.'

Mr. Emrys Hughes, Hardie's biographer,[1] points out that the reason for Hardie's bitterness on that occasion was that 250 miners had just lost their lives in a disaster in South Wales and quotes A. G. Gardiner's contemporary remark that 'Keir Hardie hated the palace because he remembered the pit'.

After the First World War Labour still maintained its revolutionary tradition and debated the republican issue. At its Annual Conference in 1923 it was presented with two republican resolutions. The first, in the words of Emrys Hughes, urged that 'the royal family is no longer a necessary part of the British constitution', and that the Labour Party should therefore 'state definitely its view of the matter'.[m] The second demanded that 'the hereditary principle in the British constitution should be abolished'. The first resolution was supported on the ground that monarchy was archaic and atrophied. The second was moved by Ernest Thurtle, George Lansbury's son-in-law, who spoke, like any nineteenth-century radical, 'as a democrat and therefore as a republican'. He suggested that Labour leaders had a 'fear complex' about the Monarchy which prevented them from saying that it was an anomaly which should be swept away.

George Lansbury, who was put up to answer for the Executive, declared that he too was a republican. But he knew there was a wide divergence of opinion on the subject in the conference 'so why fool about with an issue that has no real importance?' He had himself met members of the royal family and sat behind two princes at a football match and could assure the delegates that they were just ordinary human beings like themselves. 'When the working man had won the social revolution they would be able to do without King, Queen,

President or anyone else.' The conference agreed with him by an overwhelming majority.

When the next annual conference met the first Labour Government was in office and a much sharper controversy arose about its attitude to the Crown. Eight resolutions were tabled, sorrowing over photographs of Ramsay MacDonald and some of his colleagues, wearing 'blue gold-braided tailcoats and white kneebreeches with sword' at Buckingham Palace. The instinct of the critics that much more was involved here than a trivial issue of manners was correct. The readiness of Labour ministers to fall in with court protocol foreshadowed their future attitude to the Establishment. Not only MacDonald, but working-class members of the Government, thoroughly enjoyed the novel sensation of being received by the King, dressed as their aristocratic predecessors had been; they were glad to give the lie to newspaper charges that they were wild revolutionaries. They were Britishers who valued the traditions of their country just as much as did their social superiors.

Critics of court dress saw that their leaders were in effect accepting the role of an alternative government; they were taking the place of the decaying Liberal Party. On the platform they had presented themselves as the pioneers of a social revolution which would sweep away capitalism, class and hereditary institutions with it. Their attitude to the Monarchy, now they were in office, showed that they had never thought out the implications of revolutionary talk; when it came to the pinch they would not run the risk of open class warfare. In 1931, when told that the national economy could be saved only by lowering working-class standards, they were ready to accept office in a National Government, constitutionally arranged by the King. They had become part of the Establishment.

3

THE CONSTITUTIONAL ROLE OF
THE SOVEREIGN

WE HAVE seen that even such well-informed critics as Morley
and Dilke could believe that the Queen did almost nothing,
that she was a ceremonial cipher and that Britain was a thinly
disguised republic. The facts revealed by Queen Victoria's
letters and by a host of contemporary memoirs have shown
that her popularity, and her comparative immunity from
criticism in the latter part of her reign, were less due to her
own wisdom—she was a shrewd but not a wise woman—than
to the loyalty and chivalry of her Prime Ministers. One is
impressed first by the extraordinary amount of delay and
difficulty she caused in the conduct of government. Her correspondence over ecclesiastical appointments would by itself fill
a large book, and she exercised an important influence on
choosing the personnel who would represent Britain in foreign
countries. She was insistent in small matters and in great. She
clung to special prerogative in regard to the Army (a point
which she had learnt from Baron Stockmar), and wrote urgent
letters on questions of army dress and on the wearing of
beards in the Navy.

Until extreme old age she never relaxed her conscientious
determination to see all documents personally, even when in
days of slower communications the delay in reaching her at
Osborne or Balmoral was apt to be serious. She attempted,
with some success, to veto Cabinet appointments. In 1880,
when Gladstone had won a triumphant majority, she wrote to
Disraeli that she would 'take no notice of Mr. Gladstone, who
had done so much mischief. It is most essential that that should

Punch

The Queen dissolving Parliament, 7th August, 1847

be known.' When finally she was forced to accept Mr. Glad-stone she obstructed a number of his appointments, objecting to both Chamberlain and Dilke on the ground of their former republican opinions, and insisting on a letter of apology from Dilke before she finally accepted him as a minister. She even tried to interfere with minor government appointments, which, as Mr. Gladstone was at length driven to protest to a colleague, were submitted to her only by courtesy. Her influence on legislation was seldom important, but it is to be noticed that the Public Worship Bill was introduced at her wish and against the advice of her Prime Minister. Her activity in the Schleswig-Holstein question—her attitude here, as so often, was dictated by her memory of Prince Albert's opinions—led to a debate in the House of Lords where Lord Ellenborough, to the Queen's indignation, criticized the interference of the Crown. Her detestation of republicanism added to the difficulties of British relationships with France and the United States.

On occasions she behaved with complete disregard for the Constitution. In 1880, after a delirious period in which Disraeli had flattered her into a belief that 'the course of a Ministry depends on the will of the Queen', she found herself con-fronted with a resolute Liberal Government pledged to a number of measures which she regarded as dangerous and subversive. Her obstruction did not stop at Cabinet appoint-ments. She objected to everything; and Mr. Gladstone was compelled to remind her that the 'powerful circles in which your Majesty has active or personal intercourse' contained hardly any persons who understood the point of view of the majority of her subjects who had recently returned him to office. During the long controversy over the Sudan she expos-tulated day and night, and when Gordon was killed almost compelled Gladstone to resign by telegraphing her anger *en clair*. Her conduct on several occasions showed that she had no scruples about breaking the Constitution when she was sufficiently roused and felt safe from exposure. She wrote privately to Lady Wolseley advising Lord Wolseley, then in command of British forces in the Sudan, to coerce the Govern-ment by threatening to resign if he did not obtain the free

hand he demanded. And she urged Lady Wolseley to burn
the letter which included this advice.

In December 1885 the Queen suggested to Harcourt (while
Gladstone still had a majority) that a moderate Whig-Con-
servative coalition should be formed in order to defeat Home
Rule. Shortly afterwards, when the fall of Lord Salisbury's
first government seemed probable, she appealed to Goschen
to arrange an alliance between the Liberal Unionists and
Conservatives against Mr. Gladstone and Home Rule. In
this remarkable letter we see her surreptitiously and without
the advice of her Prime Minister attempting to promote a
'loyal' and 'constitutional' National Government in order to
defeat the Liberal Party. Nor is her correspondence with Lord
Salisbury, asking whether the Unionist Party was 'fit for an
election now' if she forced a dissolution on a Parliament with
a Liberal majority, reconcilable with even the broadest interpretation of the Monarch's constitutional functions.

Her excuse on such occasions—when she wrote to Lord
Derby about Mr. Gladstone's policy or congratulated Harcourt
on a speech attacking the Prime Minister—was that foreign
affairs and Home Rule were not 'Party questions'. But the
truth is that when the Liberals were in office the Queen never
regarded herself as bound to behave impartially or even
constitutionally. She was a vigorous woman with deep Conservative prejudices; she was the least 'impartial' of mortals
and fought against Liberalism bitterly and unscrupulously,
taking care only that her opposition should not be public
and giving way only when she had no alternative. It has
been correctly said that she used the right to 'advise' Conservative ministers or to 'warn'—I should add 'bully'—Liberal
ones.

That there was not an open scandal during Mr. Gladstone's
1880–5 ministry was due to the Prime Minister's remarkable
forbearance. The Queen complained of Palmerston's 'imperti-
nence' when he was almost eighty years old. After him no one
was left to be impertinent. Mr. Gladstone suffered from the
reverse fault. The Queen's aversion to him was personal as
well as political. True, she called him a 'mad' radical who was

ruining the country, but, even so, he might have won her personal liking if he had even understood that she was a woman as well as a queen. It was not so much that he addressed her 'as if she was a public meeting'; worse, he wrote to her as if he was a firm of lawyers and she a learned society. His labyrinthine sentences, his firstlies and sixthlies, drove her to despair. Mr. Gladstone never discovered the fact (that Disraeli knew at once by instinct) that the Queen, who by tradition had the right to demand a personal letter every day from her Prime Minister describing the events in the House of Commons, really wanted, not a reasoned memorandum, but a reassuring word that all was well with the Monarchy and the Empire. Night after night, after long hours of the most exacting labour, the indefatigable old man sat up into the small hours elaborating arguments which could have no influence with the Queen, and which were in fact often unintelligible to her.[1] No wonder that he did on one occasion privately describe her demands and her obstructionism as 'intolerable' and 'enough to kill a man'. Yet to her he was never anything but patient and courteous; his veneration for the Crown never wavered. Deeply wounded though he was, when, after a lifetime of devoted public service, the Queen accepted his resignation without a word of appreciation, sympathy or gratitude, his only request, noted in his diary, was that the details of his painful relationship with her should be kept secret. He records in his diary how he once rode all day for two or three weeks on a mule in Sicily, and concludes:

'We rode usually with little interval from 6 a.m. to 4 p.m., and its undemonstrative, unsympathetic service was not inefficiently performed. In due time we arrived at

[1] Mr. M. Macdonagh, in his book *The English King* (Benn, 1929), tells a story of the Queen which precisely illustrated her vigorous, if illogical, mind. A burglar had killed an old woman by tying a handkerchief round her mouth. Her false teeth had slipped down her throat and suffocated her. He was tried for murder and convicted. But as it was clear that the gag had been intended to silence and not to kill, the Home Secretary commuted the sentence to penal servitude. The Queen objected. 'I maintain,' she said, 'that old ladies who wear false teeth are entitled to the protection of the law.'

Messina to take our departure for the Island. There my mule and I of necessity parted company.

But I well remember having at the time a mental experience which was not unlike a turn of indigestion. I had been on the back of the beast for many scores of hours, it had done me no wrong; it had rendered me much valuable service, but it was in vain to argue; there was the fact staring me in the face. I could not get up the smallest shred of feeling for the brute; I could neither love it nor like it.

A rule of three sum is all that is necessary to conclude with. What the Sicilian mule was to me, I have been to the Queen; and the fortnight or three weeks are represented by fifty-two or fifty-three years.'

On 28 March 1881 Sir Henry Ponsonby, the Queen's Private Secretary, wrote in a letter that Gladstone had told him:

' "My day is drawing to a close. When a man gets worn out he gets gloomy. Formerly I saw no reason why Monarchy should not have gone on here for hundreds of years, but I confess that the way in which Monarchy has been brought to the front by the late government in political and foreign affairs has shaken my confidence and I dread any shock that may weaken the power of the Crown with the rising mass of politicians. Some of those you live with probably accuse me of being a radical. I am not. . . ." 'a

Characteristically, Mr. Gladstone complained not of the Queen's outrageous behaviour to himself but of the danger to the institution of monarchy implicit in Disraeli's encouragement of the Queen's autocratic temper. If he had been a radical instead of a devoted champion of tradition, Gladstone could have lighted a republican bonfire that would have consumed Buckingham Palace, Windsor Castle and Balmoral too. But he was leader of a Liberal Party in which radicals played a minor part, and he fought Disraeli without once exposing his unscrupulous use of the Crown for his own purposes.

Enough has been said to show that the Queen was ready to go behind her ministers' backs when their politics were displeasing to her. In the last resort, both in home and foreign affairs, a Prime Minister could, of course, get his own way, but often only at the expense of a lengthy and delicate combat. An important point must be added. The Queen's views were opposed to the main economic and political tendencies of the century. But she mirrored its prejudices and conventions. Her influence was usually in the direction which middle-class sentiment approved. Though she took a far more direct part in government than was generally ascribed to her, the popular conception of her character was, on the whole, remarkably accurate. She spoke, one feels, with the whole authority of her age when she refused Sir Alexander Cockburn a peerage because he had been immoral in his youth; when she opposed the idea of a Channel tunnel because 'if England is to be connected with the Continent, we shall have to keep up double the army, which we so unwillingly afford now'; when she argued against a tax on matches because it would drive some of the very poorest people and little children 'out of work'; when she declared it 'monstrous' that Mr. Gladstone should be passing laws about education instead of preventing railway accidents; when she admitted that Lord Lytton, who had provoked a war with the Afghans, had disobeyed the Cabinet in so doing, and then added: 'Now, of course, we must punish the insult, and support Lord Lytton.' When has a period ever been so accurately named as the Victorian Age?

Thus it came about that the public made her a symbol of the prosperity of their Empire, and that the prestige of the Monarchy increased when its power declined. For in spite of the Queen's tenacity and vigour, her direct part in politics inevitably grew less as she grew older. A series of powerful ministers, a firmer party organization, a growing system of civil service administration and a vast increase in the business of the State, all necessarily meant that the Queen's word counted for less in practice in the last decade of the century.

Photo: Radio Times Hulton Picture Library

The War of Attrition: George V visits a war-cemetery in Belgium

The Loyalists: a demonstration at Marble Arch

Photo: Radio Times Hulton Picture Library

In the Establishment:
Ramsay MacDonald

Denmark: The King and a bicycle

But the public neither knew nor cared for that. In her later years when the Queen appeared in public—at the Diamond Jubilee for instance—she received an overwhelming ovation. Sir Charles Dilke's discussions of her income and the once fashionable talk of republicanism were forgotten in the appearance of majesty itself. The clerk in Shoreditch felt the glamour of monarchy as keenly as the labourer in Somerset.

When the Queen died British Monarchy had won a new and personal prestige. Her great age, her perfectly representative character and the prosperity associated with her reign and the whole social tendency from *laissez-faire* Liberalism to the new popular Imperialism—all combined to stifle any breath of criticism and to endear her to her subjects. Edward VII, therefore, ascended the throne with the advantages and the disadvantages of a great, indeed an overwhelming, example to live up to. If the Queen had died twenty or thirty years earlier the history of British Monarchy might have been very different. The Queen had not then become a beloved symbol of her country as she was in 1900, and the Prince of Wales was then still considered an unsatisfactory and unstable young man who was involved in public scandals and had had to write to the Archbishop of Canterbury promising to give up his favourite game of baccarat. The middle-class public was shocked to learn about the company he kept. Even more damaging was the Mordaunt scandal, in which the Prince denied in the witness-box that he had had sexual relations with Lady Mordaunt, whose husband cited him as one of the co-respondents in his divorce suit. True, the Queen and Mr. Gladstone, as well as the jury, were avowedly satisfied with his denials. But the views of the general public, and perhaps, if the truth were known, the private views of those eminent personages, were probably more correctly interpreted by the newspaper which asked why a young married man should be so eager to pay weekly visits to a young married woman in the absence of her husband if their association 'was all that innocent'. No doubt Edward was helped by the fact that Queen Alexandra bore him five children during six years and that it is a British convention that adultery does not take place at teatime. If the

T.C.A.T.E.—E

Queen had died before Edward had had time to live down these scandals it takes no great effort of the imagination to picture a nineteenth-century abdication crisis, with Mr. Gladstone or Lord Salisbury playing the part of Mr. Baldwin. But King Edward VII had reached a comfortable middle age by the time the Queen died; the past was forgotten or accounted as the permissible sowing of royal wild oats. He had at last acquired discretion among other royal accomplishments.

For thirty years the Prince of Wales fought for the right to see Cabinet papers, but it was not until the Queen was over seventy that she gave way. She resisted every effort made on his behalf by Prime Ministers who liked Edward and wished for an experienced king. Lord Spencer and Mr. Gladstone wanted him to visit Ireland. Loyalty, they thought, would blossom wherever monarchy trod. The Queen, who bravely accepted this thesis, herself went to Ireland in her old age, but refused to allow the Prince to go, though, to be sure, she wrote saying that anything which took him 'away from the London season' would be a good thing.

In truth, the Queen, who did not willingly surrender anything, knew that the performance of public functions by the Prince would enhance his importance as well as his popularity, and this, she felt, would diminish her own prerogative.

The lack of responsibility and the failure to win a Cabinet key did not prevent Edward from gaining a general knowledge of foreign affairs; it also encouraged him to make what were regarded as 'exotic friendships' with the smart set; it consisted of 'heavy swells' and adventurers—of whom General Gallifet was typical—their snobbery, the horse-play that accompanied their dissipations, were indeed the disgusting result of total irresponsibility, idleness, utter selfishness and boredom. Politically their worst aspect was that worthless individuals were elevated because Edward wanted to do a good turn to companions who shared his pleasures.

In private life Edward found pleasure in crude forms of horse-play and committed the least pardonable of royal sins—the public humiliation of companions who were not permitted to defend themselves. Christopher Sykes has told how his uncle allowed the Prince of Wales to ruin him financially and at the same time to use him as a butt for his schoolboy idea of fun. There were not, one hopes, many hosts who would respond patiently: 'As Your Royal Highness pleases,' when the Prince poured brandy or champagne over their heads.[b] A peculiarly nauseating story of Edward at play is told by a sycophantic courtier. He relates that at a gay supper party one of the guests, having a syphon squirted over her by the Prince, quoted the famous remark of Queen Elizabeth I: 'May God forgive you, I never can.' To which the Prince of Wales gravely replied: 'That is a name which must never be used in jest.' Edward was surely the Prince of Cads.

On the other side it is fair to note that Edward, both as Prince of Wales and King, had a happy knack of making friends with men of a very different type, with Gladstone, with those former republicans, Dilke and Chamberlain, and later with some of the leaders of organized Labour. When Dilke was Under-Secretary for Foreign Affairs he kept Edward informed (as far as he dared) and put him in touch with the Local Government Board, where he managed to play a part without the Queen's intervention. As King, his public and ceremonial bearing was impeccable; he became accepted as a genial monarch who symbolized a peaceful and pleasure-loving age.

In domestic affairs much has been made of the readiness of Edward as Prince of Wales to serve on a Royal Commission on Housing and, like Sir Charles Dilke, its chairman, to pay two or three preliminary visits to slum areas. He was so far in advance of his age that he suggested that Octavia Hill should be a member of the Commission, but even her unique qualifications and the Prince's recommendation were not enough to overcome the Cabinet's prejudice against women in public affairs. The evidence given before the Commission revealed a staggering condition of filth, overcrowding and greedy landlordism. The Prince's interest was short-lived. He attended on five occasions and left to refresh himself *incognito* in Paris.

Constitutionally, he was meticulous about the royal prerogative, insisting on long explanations from ministers, complaining when Balfour in 1905 formally made the Cabinet and not the Crown responsible for the dissolution of Parliament; he also disliked being told that the Premier, and not the King, appointed and dismissed ministers. He was much annoyed when he found Balfour taking it for granted that treaties, even when they involved the cession of territory, were the business of Parliament. On such occasions he could be troublesome to ministers, but without displaying his mother's arbitrary temper.

Edward was the last British monarch to take an active and personal part in Continental politics. He was related to almost all the ruling houses of Europe and knew many of the important personages on the diplomatic stage. If the title of Peacemaker meant anything, it is that he helped to swing opinion on to the side of the new *Entente* with France by tactful behaviour during a timely visit to Paris, and that his detestation of his bombastic nephew, the Kaiser, and his love for France (often confused with his addiction to the Moulin Rouge) tended to keep relations with France sweet and to embitter British rivalry with Germany.

The legend of his influence in foreign affairs seems to have been born after his death. It was a theme of his obituary writers, and is well illustrated by a broadsheet sold at his funeral. To the historian of opinion such broadsheets have the special interest of spontaneity and illiteracy. Here are the two last verses:

> Greatest sorrow England ever had
> When death took away our dear Dad:
> A King was he from head to sole
> Loved by his people one and all.
>
> His mighty work for the Nation
> Making peace and strengthening Union—
> Always at it since on the throne:
> Saved the country more than one billion.[c]

The first important constitutional crisis of Edward's reign began only shortly before his death. In the summer of 1909 it became clear that the House of Lords intended to throw out

Lloyd George's Land Budget, and that Asquith was equally determined to force the House of Lords to give way, and, if necessary, permanently to curtail its powers.[d] The issue that dominated British politics during the next five years was whether the remnants of hereditary power vested in the Crown and the House of Lords would survive in democratic England. In the event the House of Lords survived, shorn of much of its power, and the Monarchy came through with enhanced prestige.

The whole complex story of the relations between the Crown and the Liberal leaders can today be pieced together from memoirs and published documents. The student of these often contradictory and involved narratives, full of a life-and-death bitterness which comes as a surprise to this generation, will be impressed by the persistence with which the Tories throughout assumed that the King must always be on the side of the Conservative Party and that it was his duty, within the widest interpretation of the Constitution, to uphold privilege and block the progress of radical reforms. Some of the King's closest advisers made the same assumption, but, being prudent and experienced men, they were conscious of the danger that the wilder spirits in the Tory Party might push the Monarch along a path that would lead him into open conflict with the Liberal Party and the majority of the electorate.

The British Constitution is fluid; the nominal powers of the Monarch are large and the zone of discretion undefined. In practice the powers of the King are limited by precedent and by the lessons of history—from Charles I downwards. He is subject to the paramount consideration that, if he rejects the advice of his Prime Minister, he may well find himself without a government and, like the Stuarts or William IV, come into conflict with social forces that may threaten the throne.

George V was not a clever man, and his education was that of a naval officer. He was uncomplicated and religious, conscientious, honest and rather timid. He wanted always 'to do the right thing'. Though he had a very adequate appreciation of royal dignity, he was not tempted to follow his grand-mother's example and make life a burden to his ministers.

The Monarchy never came into conflict with the electorate on any of the constitutional issues of his reign because the King and his private advisers were prudently anxious not to embroil the Crown in party politics, while the pre-war Liberal leaders and the post-war Labour reformers were all loyalists, anxious to help the King in his difficulties. Perhaps most important of all, the Ulster crisis, constitutionally far the most dangerous, was averted by the outbreak of the European war.

Four main constitutional crises severely tested the value and the powers of the Monarchy during the reign of George V. The first, the Budget dispute with the House of Lords in 1909–10, had already taken shape before the death of Edward VII. It merged almost at once into the second, and more important, House of Lords dispute which ended with the passing of the Parliament Act in 1911. The third crisis came to a head with the Curragh Mutiny in 1914. The fourth was due to the collapse of the Labour Government of 1931.

The 1909 crisis arose from the Lords' rejection of the Budget in November and Asquith's motion in the Commons declaring that their refusal to pass a financial measure was 'a breach of the Constitution and a usurpation of the rights of the Commons'. The Prime Minister followed this with a declaration at the opening of the general election campaign that the Liberals would not again take office 'unless we can secure safeguards which experience shows us to be necessary' —a phrase which meant that he demanded assurances from the King that enough peers would be created to overcome obstruction by the House of Lords. The precise attitude of the Crown at this juncture is on record. Lord Knollys, one of the King's private secretaries, informed Asquith's Private Secretary that the King 'regards the policy of the Government as tantamount to the destruction of the House of Lords and he thinks that before a large creation of peers is embarked upon or threatened, the country should be acquainted with the particular project for accomplishing such destruction, as well as with the general line of action as to which the country will be consulted at the forthcoming elections'.

In the election that followed the Liberals were returned

with a majority of only two over the Conservatives, but with a
working majority of Irish and Labour supporters. How the
situation looked to one of the ablest of the Monarch's un-
official advisers we know from the published letters of Lord
Esher. He had urged the King to refuse to create peers before
the general election, saying that 'if the government resigned,
because of this refusal, the King would be supported by this
country and all over the Empire'. In an illuminating letter to
his son, however, Lord Esher wrote: 'About February 10th.
the Prime Minister will be asking the King for a promise to
create peers. That is *certain*. If the King says yes, he mortally
offends the whole Tory Party to which he is naturally bound.
If he says no, he lets loose all the Radical gutter press at his
position as sovereign and his person as a man. A charming
dilemma, full of revolutionary possibilities. We have never
been nearer a revolution since 1688. . . .'e

The result of the Lords' opposition was to hold up the
Budget for one year. They passed it without a division on
28 April 1910. In the same month the Archbishop of Canterbury held an informal conference at Lambeth Palace to discuss
the King's dilemma. It was attended by Lord Esher, Balfour,
Leader of the Opposition, and Lord Knollys, the King's
Private Secretary. The Archbishop reported that the King
had already discussed his difficulty with him. Balfour held that
if the King should refuse a promise to create peers, he

'should do so in a carefully worded document—so carefully worded as to show no bias towards either party
or policy, and that this document should be read by the
Prime Minister in parliament. The Archbishop observed
that the difficulty of formulating such a document lay in
the well-nigh impossibility of avoiding the Scylla of appearing to side with the Unionist Party and not falling into
the Charybdis of appearing to dance to the Liberal pipe, by
saying beforehand that he would acquiesce, if a Liberal
majority was returned to parliament. Mr. Balfour said
that it would require care, but that in his opinion a satisfactory document could be framed and, if successfully framed,

would add much lustre to the position of the Sovereign. He pointed out that if the King refused the Prime Minister's proposal, the Government would resign, and that he, Mr. Balfour, would then form a Government and immediately ask the King to grant him a dissolution.'f

This was Lord Esher's summary. Lord Knollys also made a note of Balfour's characteristically balanced statement. Edward VII died shortly afterwards and Knollys never told George V of Balfour's view.

After the short truce that followed the old King's death another constitutional conference met, but without result. Asquith reminded the King that he might be asked to coerce the Lords by the threat of creating peers as William IV had been compelled to do in 1832. The argument now turned on whether the Prime Minister had the right to extract from the King a promise about his conduct if the Government were returned with a majority in favour of a parliament Bill restricting the powers of the House of Lords. Ought the King to be asked for a 'contingent guarantee'? In the end the King agreed, in his own words, 'most reluctantly', to give the Government a secret undertaking, and it was this undertaking which, when finally read to the House of Lords by Lord Morley, defeated the 'last-ditchers' and induced the Lords to vote for their own emasculation.

Balfour did not forgive Knollys for his reticence, and George V, when he learnt of Balfour's statement three years later, suggested that he might have made a different decision if he had known that Balfour was available at the time. But it seems very doubtful whether Balfour would in fact have formed a government in these circumstances, and equally doubtful whether the King would have been wise to ask him to do so. However subtly the constitutional issue might have been presented by Balfour, the election would inevitably have turned into a struggle between the Liberal Party, challenging the right of the Lords to block reformist legislation, and the Conservatives, using the name of the King to defeat it.

The danger of involving the King in party politics was here, as throughout his reign, the decisive factor. This danger was inherent in any personal action by the King not expressly authorized by the Premier. The one form of personal initiative permitted him—and it was deeply comforting to him in his anxieties—was to seek accommodation through inter-party conferences. He resorted to it, with the Premier's agreement, in the struggle with the Lords and again in the Ulster crisis. There were also ample precedents during Queen Victoria's reign for the Monarch having private interviews with Opposition leaders in times of crisis, provided that the Prime Minister knew that he was doing so and was informed of the substance of the conversations. On one critical occasion, when the King wished to talk with the Tory leaders, Asquith reluctantly agreed only after sending the King a memorandum drawing a distinction between 'seeking advice' and 'desiring knowledge' from the Opposition. The King accepted the distinction and did not attempt to act as arbiter. As it turned out, Asquith was justified in his fear that an attempt would be made at this interview to divert the issue and weaken the King's resolution. But the King seems to have realized that the only safe and constitutional course for him in all such talks was to make it clear that he would follow the Premier's advice.

The one occasion when the King might have been persuaded to depart from this simple and safe rule was during the Ulster crisis of 1913. The King was particularly vulnerable on this issue, because he felt deeply that the proposal to give Home Rule to Catholic Ireland involved his oath as a Protestant monarch; because the Ulster men and their Tory backers in England were often personal friends and 'members of the Carlton Club'; because he was revolted at the idea of breaking up his imperial domains and giving way to Irish nationalists. He was desperately and justifiably anxious to prevent a civil war in which the Army would be divided in its loyalties and his government compelled to coerce those politicians with whom his personal sympathies lay. He was beset by a large correspondence, much of it anonymous, from people who were sure that he wouldn't 'hand over Ulster to the Pope'. Moreover, his usually cautious advisers proved ready to argue that the normal constitutional rules did not apply when a change in the structure of the Empire was contemplated. Lord Esher, for instance, went so far as to argue that in this special case the King's duty was to dismiss his government even though it had a large majority behind it. It was this type of advice, hidden but influential, that justified the radical press of the time in declaring that 'court hangers-on' were bringing pressure on the King, and it was with such occasions in mind that Sir Stafford Cripps was later to get into trouble for speaking of obstruction from 'Buckingham Palace circles'.

The King had to listen to a legion of unwise voices. Lord Halsbury and Bonar Law not only supported the treasonable utterances of Lord Carson, F. E. Smith and Joynson-Hicks, but actually committed themselves to the dangerous proposition that the King still had a veto and should use it. The diaries of Sir Henry Wilson show that there were soldiers recklessly ready to promote a civil war and to argue that they were obeying the personal wishes of His Majesty against those of his government. It was natural in these circumstances that Liberal politicians and Liberal newspapers should have regarded with suspicion the King's attempt to settle matters at a Buckingham Palace conference.

The European war ended the Ulster crisis, and the King did not in fact yield to reckless advice. That there was real danger that his judgment might be swayed is clear, however, from a conversation he had with Asquith in February 1914. It occurred at the moment when the Prime Minister, with a Parliamentary majority behind him, was in the throes of a formidable struggle to get his Home Rule measure passed. He had to make it acceptable to Redmond and his Irish supporters and hoped to avoid civil war with the Ulster rebels and their disloyal British supporters. Yet the King, who liked and respected Asquith personally, was so alarmed by Tory and Ulster threats that he talked about the advantage of a general election to 'clear the air' and to 'show whether the Government really had a mandate for Home Rule'. He even went on to say that, at a later stage, he might 'feel it his duty to do what in his own judgment was best for the people generally'. This, as Asquith at once saw, meant that the King was at least toying with the idea of resurrecting the royal veto—which was, literally, as Asquith remarked, as dead as Queen Anne. The Prime Minister's remonstrance seems to have been enough to kill this idea, but the incident remains as a warning that unscrupulous politicians may appeal to the personal loyalty of soldiers and sailors to the Crown against the Government which represents the electorate whose servants the King, the Government and the armed forces alike must be.

An extraordinary divergence of views still existed in 1913 about the powers remaining to the Sovereign. In the crisis of 1913 many 'elder statesmen' were called in to give advice. All of them, Lord Oxford's biographers remark, 'strove to be impartial, but as the records show, their views of what the Crown might do were generally in accord with what they wished it to do'.[g] Lord Lansdowne took the extreme line that since the Parliament Act had destroyed the power of the Lords to kill a Bill, the power reverted to the Crown: the King, in his opinion, could force a dissolution or insist on a referendum. Bonar Law held that the King could dismiss his ministers, even though they had a Parliamentary majority, dissolve Parliament and ascertain the popular will. In the opposite camp Lord Rosebery and Lord Oxford were, of course, sure that it was unconstitutional for the King to reject the Premier's advice.

It has been held that George V did in fact refuse Asquith a dissolution in 1911, and it is true that the King accepted his advice only after Asquith had agreed to introduce the Parliament Act into the Lords before announcing a dissolution. But to argue that the King, on this occasion, rejected the Premier's advice seems a strained interpretation. No one doubts that the King has the right to give as well as take advice and to urge his desires on the Premier; in this case Asquith acceded to the King's desire without demur. There was no conflict of wills such as is implied in speaking of the King rejecting the Premier's advice.

The last occasion when the King had changed a ministry

which still had a majority in the country was in 1834; the result, as might be expected, was wholly detrimental to the Crown, which had to accept defeat and to yield to a triumphant Parliamentary majority. The lesson of refusals by governor-generals—in Canada by Lord Byng in 1925, and by Sir Andrew Duncan in South Africa in 1939—is similar; it it is also discouraging to those who argue that a dissolution is a matter for the King's personal decision, and it may safely be asserted that the experiment in the Dominions is quite unlikely to be repeated. If the King insists on an election against the Prime Minister's advice—or indeed does anything else to thwart the will of the Party with a House of Commons majority—he is taking sides, his position as impartial Head of the State disappears, with the inevitable result that the election will turn on the King's interference and that the republican issue will be raised. For the Monarch the only safe rule is always to follow the Premier's advice once it is given. His one right—just as it would be a president's in any European republic—is to argue the matter out in private and compel the Prime Minister to give reasons for his decision.

Several other constitutional controversies have since then arisen which seem to me to confirm, not to throw doubt on, the universal applicability of this rule. On one issue—the choice of a new Prime Minister, when there is doubt about the leadership of the Party with the largest Parliamentary representation—the outgoing Prime Minister may not be considered the proper person to give advice. For the Sovereign to make a personal decision on such occasions does not bring him into the field of Party warfare, and there is, in fact, no doubt that in this situation the King has the right of individual choice. King George was personally responsible for entrusting the formation of a new Conservative Government in 1923 to Mr. Baldwin, rather than to Lord Curzon, just as Queen Victoria was personally responsible for summoning Lord Rosebery in 1896.

The same question arose when Sir Anthony Eden retired in 1957. Since it was uncertain who was the Tory leader, it was, theoretically at least, the Queen's personal decision to send for Mr. Macmillan rather than Mr. Butler. Mr. Randolph Churchill's assertion that the choice was in fact made by Lord Salisbury, with the knowledge and agreement of only a few other leading Tories, raised a storm inside the Conservative Party. The complaint was not that the choice had not been left to the Queen, but that the Party should have been allowed to choose its own leader—a position that is now explicitly laid down in the Labour Party's constitution. It follows that in practice such a personal choice by the Monarch is now likely always to be only a formality. The Party with the majority in the House of Commons will in effect decide the new Prime Minister by its own choice of leader.

A more interesting question arose in 1924 when Asquith, as leader of the Liberal Party, in the House of Commons, displayed the frailty of human nature by urging that, in the conditions of three-party government, the King had the right to refuse a dissolution to the defeated Prime Minister and to call upon leaders of other parties to attempt to form a government. Surely the fundamental principle, which he himself laid down in 1913, applied here too. If the King had refused MacDonald a dissolution and called upon Asquith to form a government, the result would have been to proclaim the King a partisan and to bring him into the Party arena. The result might well have been better for the Labour Party, but it would certainly have been disastrous for the Monarchy.

About another incident, the part played by the Monarchy in arranging the National Government in 1931, the memoirs of persons still alive continue to raise doubts. Lord Parmoor declared that the King's action was definitely unconstitutional. It was undoubtedly a serious innovation, as Professor Laski and others have pointed out, that a Prime Minister, who must hold his position in virtue of the fact that he is the leader of the largest Party in the House of Commons, should form a new government without the consent, or even the knowledge, of his own Party. We know today that manœuvres for forming a National Government had been proceeding for months before the actual crisis in August 1931. And we know from his Private Secretary's memoranda that the King played an important part in the final arrangements. But the King had the right to advise, and even if the arrangement which had brought together MacDonald, Baldwin and Sir Herbert Samuel was actually managed by the King or members of his immediate entourage, I can scarcely see that he was behaving unconstitutionally. I can see danger in such manœuvres, but I do not see that the King exceeded his duties. Constitutionally, he must be presumed to have been taking his Prime Minister's advice. We may demand that the King should always subordinate his own will on public issues to the will of the Prime Minister, but we cannot demand that he should exercise no influence on the Prime Minister's decision. That would be to demand that the King should have no opinions and no personality; that, in spite of continuous experience of political life that may well be longer than that of the Prime Minister, he should be no more than a 'rubber stamp'.

Similar considerations seem to apply to the part played by the King in the appointment of Ernest Bevin and not Dr. Hugh Dalton as Foreign Secretary in 1945. The agreed facts are that Attlee went to the Palace on the evening of 26 July and mentioned Dalton's name as Foreign Secretary. The King, as Wheeler-Bennett tells us, recorded in his diary: 'I disagreed with him and said that foreign affairs was the most important subject at the moment and hoped he would make Mr. Bevin take it. He said he would.' Sir A. Lascelles added in his own diary—it was King George VI's habit to inform his Private Secretary of what had passed in important interviews—that 'Mr. Attlee mentioned to the King that he was thinking of appointing Mr. Dalton to be his Foreign Secretary. His Majesty begged him to think carefully about this and suggested that Mr. Bevin would be a better choice.' Commenting on this account, Earl Attlee himself argued that Wheeler-Bennett had made too much of the incident and continued: 'I was at first inclined to put Mr. Dalton at the Foreign Office—as he had been Under-Secretary in 1929—and make Mr. Bevin Chancellor, since he had served on the Macmillan Committee and was well versed in finance. I don't recollect that the King expressed any very strong views on the subject, but he seemed inclined to prefer Mr. Bevin as Foreign Secretary. After the audience I reconsidered the matter and decided that it would be better to put Mr. Bevin at the Foreign Office.' Attlee explains that Bevin and Morrison did not get on well together and that it was essential to give them 'spheres of action where there was not so much opportunity for a clash of personalities'. In his own account of the incident, clearly written without knowledge of the evidence produced by Wheeler-Bennett, Dr. Dalton argued that the rumours that the King had influenced Attlee's decision were untrue, since Attlee had told him he would almost certainly go to the Foreign Office on the morning of the 27th after Attlee had seen the King the previous evening. He believes that Attlee's final decision at four o'clock that afternoon was due to his conviction that Bevin and Morrison must be kept apart. Summarizing this story, it seems clear that the King's advice was one of the factors that made Attlee change his mind, but there is no ground for suggesting that he brought any improper pressure to bear on the Premier.[h]

There are two instances in which everyone today would agree that George V justifiably used his personal right to protest and warn. The first concerned the treatment of suffragettes in gaol. The incident of the débutante who actually dared to speak —and to speak loudly—to the King when she was presented at court is largely forgotten today. But it is a fact that one of the young women said, as she curtsied: 'Will your Majesty stop the torture of women?'—or words to that effect. She was hustled out by horrified officials. Whether her words affected the King is not known. We do know, however, that when the cat-and-mouse Bill was drafted by a government exasperated by Mrs. Pankhurst's militant tactics, Lord Stamfordham, the King's principal Private Secretary, wrote to Mr. McKenna, the Home Secretary:

'The King desires me to write to you upon the question of "forcible feeding". His Majesty cannot help feeling that there is something shocking, if not almost cruel, in the operation to which these insensate women are subjected through their refusal to take necessary nourishment. His

Majesty concludes that Miss Pankhurst's description of what she endured when forcibly fed is more or less true. If so, her story will horrify people otherwise not in sympathy with the Militant Suffragettes. The King asks whether, in your "Temporary Discharge of Prisons Bill" it would not be possible to abolish forcible feeding.'i

In the barbarous mid-twentieth century, when we are hardened to reading about the atrocious acts committed by many governments in their determination to 'maintain law and order', the King's concern about the forcible feeding of women in gaol makes agreeable reading. The second incident, in which the King protested at measures taken by his ministers, is a further proof of his detestation of cruelty. He even disliked cruelty to rebellious subjects. Throughout the Irish struggle his aim was to prevent violence, and after the war, when Bonar Law's government was, to put it bluntly and truthfully, waging war against the united people of Southern Ireland, the King repeatedly instructed his Private Secretary to write to his ministers asking what the Government 'intended to do towards further protecting the lives of unoffending people in Ireland'. The answers he got from Bonar Law and the new Chief Secretary for Ireland—men have never lied more continuously to the House of Commons—were each time to the effect that the Irish Government 'must take whatever measures were necessary to maintain law and order', and that the Republican movement was 'crumbling' as the result of our gallant military action. The King, however, as Sir Harold Nicolson remarks, 'regarded himself—it was an honourable illusion—as the protector of his Irish as well as his British subjects'. He protested at the arbitrary behaviour of the military in Ireland and in particular rejected the whole philosophy of reprisals. In July 1921 a newspaper in the U.S. published a supposed interview with Northcliffe, who was represented as saying that the King was opposed to the Government's Irish policy and had protested against the reprisal policy of the Black and Tans. Lloyd George told the Commons that the whole thing was 'a complete fabrication', but, says Nicolson, 'however unauthorized the interview, it was not in fact a fanciful presentation of the King's feeling at the time. He certainly expressed the view that the Black and Tans should be disbanded and the constabulary should be subjected to military discipline under the command of Sir Nevil Macready.'

In one other field George V tried to maintain a personal initiative and the right to refuse the Premier's wishes. The Monarch, as the traditional phrase has it, is the fountain of honour. Which does not mean, as Edward VII objected, that it is a pump. That certainly would be a fair description of Lloyd George's use of the royal prerogative to buy support for himself. Doubtful friends and likely enemies might be bought by making them baronets, barons or even viscounts. He sold honours at a price, and the amount that had to be paid to his personal or party fund for a place in the peerage became known and created a scandal, which was one of the reasons for his fall from power in 1922. George V was furious. We find him writing, through Lord Stamfordham, urging Lloyd George not to raise the question of Lord Rothermere's promotion to the peerage. Rothermere, he said, had not done well as Air Minister; he had been made a Privy Councillor 'which in itself is a high distinction'. Another letter was written by Stamfordham to Frederick Guest, Coalition Chief Whip, who arranged these little matters for Lloyd George, saying that 'the King certainly has no recollection' of any suggestion of Rothermere's elevation being submitted to him. Bonar Law had to intervene and explain that Rothermere had been told that he would become a peer and 'it would create a very unpleasant position if His Majesty could not see his way to accept the recommendation'.

The King had to give his approval 'but with much reluctance'. He was even more reluctant about a number of other nominations. Lord Beaverbrook tells us that his own promotion to the Lords 'provoked a tremendous storm'. On this occasion Stamfordham wrote to Lloyd George that His Majesty 'was surprised and hurt that this honour should have been offered without first obtaining his consent . . .

the King recognizes (in view of the promises made and information given) that it is impossible for him now to withhold his approval. But, in thus signifying his acquiescence, His Majesty commands me to say that he feels the Sovereign's Prerogative should not be disregarded; and he trusts that in future no honours whatever will be offered by any minister until his approval has been informally obtained. His Majesty further asks that this be made clear to your colleagues.'

The King also put up unavailing fights against the appointment of other press lords, in particular that of Lord Riddell, the proprietor of the *News of the World*. Lord Beaverbrook explains that the trouble in this case was that Riddell had been divorced. The story does not end there, however, for in at least one case in which Lloyd George wanted to sell a peerage to a disreputable millionaire, the King objected and sustained his objection. Another interesting instance in which the King proved himself no rubber stamp had occurred many years before. Ramsay MacDonald had incautiously promised a peer of no particular distinction that he would be made Viceroy of India. The offer leaked to George V, who promptly sent for MacDonald and told him that he would not consent. In this case it was the Prime Minister who gave way.

If that were the whole story Edward VII and George V would stand assured as exemplary models of constitutional monarchs. But the King in England has another, less publicized, role, which springs from his position as head of the Establishment. By the nature of our society, monarchs are surrounded by an exclusive set of persons, drawn almost wholly from the aristocracy; some of them will be service officers they have known at Sandhurst or when they were training as naval cadets. During the Ulster crisis, as we have seen, King George's personal ties with a small circle of Conservative advisers and top-ranking soldiers made it difficult and embarrassing for him properly to preserve his constitutional relations with the Premier. Recent publications have revealed that during the First World War he used his personal influence in a way that must be deeply disturbing to advocates of constitutional monarchy. It must remain a matter of argument and speculation among military historians whether the King's secret support of Haig prolonged the war; that it added greatly to the number of young Englishmen who died in it seems probable. What is certain is that it amounted to a very important exercise of personal power that is not included in official accounts of the role of Constitutional Monarchy. It provides a perfect example of the Monarch's unpublicized influence as head of the Establishment. The story demands a chapter to itself.

4

THE CROWN AND THE ESTABLISHMENT

ONLY a few years ago if one had said that the Monarch was head of the Establishment it would have meant that he was Defender of the Faith and Head of the Protestant Church as established in Britain in the sixteenth century and perpetuated in the seventeenth by the Act of Settlement. The present generation means something more than this by the Establishment, but usually something very imprecise.

Angry Young Men who inveigh against it seem often to mean no more than that the career is still not equally open to the talents; that they are handicapped in the race for positions which influence so quickly wins for less gifted men. They resent the part that privilege still plays in education; that Eton, Harrow and Winchester, Oxford and Cambridge are straight roads to the best jobs, while special talent is required from the products of less famous schools and red-brick universities. Some people have a pull that is not publicly recognized or sanctioned. It must have been an anti-Establishment versifier who wrote:

> The halls of life are always full,
> The doors are always ajar,
> And some get in by the door marked push
> And some by the door marked pull.

Probably the best definition of the Establishment is that it is that part of our government that has not been subjected to democratic control. It is the combined influence of persons who play a part in public life, though they have not been appointed on any public test of merit or election. More important still, they are not subject to dismissal by democratic process. They uphold a tradition and form a core of continuity in our institutions. They are privileged persons and their positions are not as a rule affected by changes of government. It is untrue to say, as some impetuously do, that their existence makes democracy a humbug, but the more detailed knowledge we have of the daily working of our system, the clearer it is that much that the public assumes to be decided by their elected representatives is really managed by persons whose names may not even be known to the public.

The Monarch stands at the apex of this unpublicized part of the state machine. The King is the centre of its loyalty and the link between the changing, democratic institutions and its permanent, privately operating ones. The vast publicity which the Monarch personally receives helps to preserve the discreet silence that surrounds most of the proceedings of the Establishment.

Who then compose it? Standing immediately near to the Monarch are members of the royal family in all their many ramifications. Then there is the inner circle of private and Cabinet secretaries—persons of incalculable influence—of whom the public seldom hears; there are also traditional officers, including the Lord High Steward, his deputies and staff, who, except on certain ceremonial occasions, are never publicly mentioned at all. There are also members of great families who have played an important public or private part in politics for many generations; the Salisbury family is an outstanding illustration. Elder statesmen may qualify by long service and archbishops and senior bishops, who have been appointed by the Crown, are included as trustees of religious orthodoxy. The Governor of the Bank of England and his colleagues are appointed as trustees of financial orthodoxy; similarly, in all probability and intention, the editor of *The Times* and the Director General of the B.B.C. will be appointed as trustworthy supporters of institutional orthodoxy. Other recruits are senior Civil Servants, who form natural members of the Establishment, as well as the Service chiefs, their staffs and inner circle of Intelligence and Secret Service officers.

It will be seen that the core of the Establishment is still aristocratic. But it has always been the strength of the British ruling class that it has been recruited from outside. Recruits, who may not be qualified by birth, may arrive within the inner circle because they have achieved by the democratic process positions of power which makes their co-operation essential to the Establishment. That this continues to work smoothly today is due to the fact that even after two world wars and six years of Labour government from 1945 to 1951, the most important posts still go to those who have been to the right schools and universities. They share a set of convictions and prejudices which may be matters of laughter and dispute in private, but which are accepted in public and which in a crisis prove decisive.

In a fluid society, which is based on a Parliamentary and representative system, the Prime Minister and his senior colleagues are inevitably incorporated in the Establishment. One way of ensuring that an influential politician will not revolt against it is to make him a Privy Councillor; the Leader of the Opposition is in effect co-opted by receiving a substantial salary. The Monarch plays an essential part in holding this system together. He or she is the one person to whom all intimate quarrels and controversies at the top, officially secret, level may legitimately be made known. Either personally or through private secretaries, the Monarchy is the depository of much highly confidential information, and it may be its job to smooth out disharmonies within the Establishment. The Monarchy may act as the final arbiter when there appears danger of a breach in the continuity of government.

Occasionally it happens that the political parties clash on a basic issue that divides the Establishment. The House of Lords and Irish issues nearly brought England to civil war in 1913–14, and on all such occasions constitutional usage entitles the Monarch to seek a settlement in a conference which he may personally summon and even preside over. But political controversy in this country does not often reach a point at which the Monarch may publicly intervene. What Beatrice Webb used to call 'the aristocratic embrace' is usually effective in maintaining a non-revolutionary atmosphere in Parliament. Comparatively few M.P.s who arrive at Westminster with revolution on their lips and fire in their bellies prove intractable to the proper Establishment treatment. The most feared and disliked revolutionaries—rare birds in this country—are persons like Sir Stafford Cripps who come themselves from ruling families and are not cheated into mistaking the small change of courtesy for the reality of concession or victory. It was not an accident that Sir Stafford was bitterly pursued by the Tory press in the heated days of the Popular Front and the Spanish War. He knew what he was talking about when he attacked 'Buckingham Palace circles'; they existed and he recognized them as powerful enemies of the causes in which he then believed. If he later himself became a highly respected member of the Establishment it was not because he was flattered by invitations to Cliveden or the temptations of office; it was because the circumstances of war and its aftermath offered full scope for his abilities and ambition.

Modern English history offers few more instructive topics of study than the methods used by the Establishment for taming or rendering harmless M.P.s who expect to continue at Westminster to fight for the revolutionary causes they had championed in their constituencies. The life of David Kirkwood, as written by himself, reveals in all its simplicity how a bold and sincere man, who thought himself an uncompromising revolutionary, ended up in the House of Lords, and became an enthusiastic monarchist after meeting the Prince of Wales. Of the group of Clydesiders, who sounded so frightening when they invaded London after the First World War, James Maxton, who would not dine with the rich, was rendered ineffective by being praised and petted as a great orator to whom everybody listened, but who was by hypothesis not to be taken seriously. Possibly Wheatley, the ablest of these Scottish socialists, might have withstood the impact of courtesy and tradition which overwhelmed his colleagues. He died before the issue was put to the test, but not before he put it on record that having seen the Establishment at work he thought it not worth while attacking the Crown since it would disappear in the coming social revolution.

The wisdom of the British ruling class has seldom been better expressed than by Richard Haldane (later Lord Haldane) who wrote a manifesto (published in the *Sunday Times*, December 1923) pleading with Liberals and Conservatives to give Labour a fair opportunity at trying its hand at government.[a]

> 'We have to recognize that a great change is in progress. Labour has attained to commanding power and to a new status. There is no need for alarm. All may go well if as a nation we keep in mind the necessity of the satisfaction of two new demands—that for the recognition of the title to equality, and for more knowledge and its systematic application to industry and to the rest of life. We have not yet fully awakened to the necessity for recognizing and meeting either of these demands. The result of the General Election may prove a blessing to us if it has awakened us to our neglect of something momentous which has been slowly emerging for years past. . . . Three quarters of a century since, the old Whigs, wise in their limited way, refused to meet the Chartist movement merely with a blank refusal. Thereby they earned our gratitude. For while most of the nations of Europe were plunged into revolution as a result of turning deaf ears to their violent progressives, we were saved, and remained in comparative quiet. . . . We had spoken with the enemy in the gate, and he had turned out to be of the same flesh and blood as ourselves. . . .'

Consistently with this advice, Haldane accepted office in Ramsay MacDonald's first administration. He joined as Lord Chancellor and—the addition, as we shall see, was of vital importance—he was also permitted to 'take an active part in the deliberations of the Committee of Imperial Defence'.

Haldane proved right. There was no cause for alarm. George V was immensely relieved to find that the first Labour

Prime Minister had himself an Establishment mind and had appointed an Establishment man to watch over Defence. The senior members of the Administration were flattered, overwhelmed, by the affability of the King and very ready to cooperate with the Establishment in keeping their Left Wing in order.

When the second Labour Government (1929–31) was confronted with the dilemma of either adopting a socialist policy, which it had never seriously thought out, or of joining forces with the Conservatives, MacDonald, Snowden and Thomas unhesitatingly chose the second course. The story of Ramsay MacDonald's second administration provides the best possible illustration of Lord Balfour's dictum that whatever Party is in office, the Conservatives are always in power.

Anyone who wishes to obtain a detailed picture of the Establishment at work over a number of years and to estimate the part which the Monarchy plays in it is compelled to go back to the period before the First World War. One reason for this is the fifty years' ban imposed by the Foreign Office on the publication of official records. The letters of royalty are only published with the most careful discrimination many years after they are written and it takes a recalcitrant statesman like Lloyd George to carry off Cabinet documents and publish them on his own authority and in spite of governmental warning. Again it takes a rogue elephant like Beaverbrook, with a vast private fortune and a deep grudge against the Establishment, to lay bare in intimate detail the secrets of Cabinet intrigues, in which he himself played an important part, during the lifetime of leading personalities who might be annoyed by the breach of secrecy.

I propose to take two examples of the influence of the Monarchy from the period before and during the First World War. It is possible to do this in some detail because we have at our disposal the four volumes of *The Journals and Letters of Reginald, Viscount Esher*, the *Private Papers of Douglas Haig* and *Men and Power* by Lord Beaverbrook.

Although the most secret of Lord Esher's journals and letters are said to have been withheld from publication, the extracts that are published supply superb material for those who wish to understand how the British Establishment works. Each volume contains a synopsis of Esher's career, recording that he went to Eton and Cambridge, was Private Secretary to Lord Hartington from 1878 to 1885, that he refused invitations to edit both the *Daily News* and *New Review*; that among a long list of other refusals he rejected offers to be Under-Secretary for the Colonies, Under-Secretary for War and Governor of Cape Colony; that he also refused to be Secretary of State for War and declined to be a G.C.B. in 1905—an honour he accepted three years later. More remarkable, he refused to be Viceroy of India in 1908. The jobs he did not refuse were Keeper of the King's Archives and membership of the Royal Commission on the South African War; he was a permanent member of the Committee for Imperial Defence and Chairman of the Committee that organized the Territorial Army; he became a Privy Councillor, Governor of Windsor Castle and Chairman of the Committee on the organization of the Indian Army. He refused an earldom.

This record makes it clear that Lord Esher had no wish for notoriety and one understands why his son, in editing his journals and letters, includes on the title page of each volume the following quotation from Lord Beaconsfield: 'The most powerful men are not public men. The public man is responsible, and the responsible man is a slave. It is private life that governs the world.'

The secret of Esher's power was his intimacy with Edward VII and, to a lesser extent afterwards, with George V. Esher advised Edward VII upon all matters of state, but more particularly about the Army and Defence, which were still regarded as peculiarly within the province of the Crown. He saw that the disastrous conduct of the Boer War had revealed, as every successive war in our history has done, that our Service Chiefs had no professional understanding of the job of war and no notion of keeping up to date with military science.

Balfour's administration from 1901 to 1905 was a signal failure. Its one achievement was unknown to the public. With the help of Lord Esher and the warm support of the King, a Committee of Defence was set up to co-ordinate and plan the work of the Chiefs of Staff and work out their needs in terms of ships, weapons and manpower. It had scarcely begun its work when the unpopularity of the Government seemed to threaten its existence. The 'Balfour Must Go' slogan was clearly about to achieve its object. What, Esher asked, would happen to the new committee if it was deprived of the 'protecting arm of Balfour'? What indeed was to be expected when a Little Englander like Campbell-Bannerman became Premier, with colleagues like Lloyd George, a pro-Boer and radical Reformer, not to mention Winston Churchill, who was then implacably intent on cutting the military estimates?

The King was fully alive to the danger to the committee, and on 5 October 1905 discussed the subject at Balmoral with his Private Secretary, Lord Knollys, Balfour (still Prime Minister), Lord Esher and Mr. Richard Haldane. The remarkable fact was the inclusion of Haldane, a young Liberal M.P. who had made a name for himself at the Bar and was regarded as omniscient about many things, including Germany—where he had, in fact, been for only a few months a student. He was known to be deeply interested in military affairs and he belonged to the small Liberal imperialist group, which included Asquith and Grey.

On 7 September 1906 Esher wrote to the Duchess of Sutherland:

'There is a very bad time coming for soldiers; for the laws of historical and ethnographical evolution (it sounds rather priggish) require that we shall fight one of the most powerful military empires that has ever existed.

This is *certain*, and we have a very short period for preparation. I feel that proficiency in games, or in the hunting-field, will not help our poor lads much when they have to face the carefully trained and highly educated German officers.'

He tried hard to convince his colleagues—as early as 1906—
that we were no longer 'an Island state' and that conscription
was necessary for defence.

At this meeting it was decided that the best way to meet the
danger was to set up two permanent sub-committees which
would function undisturbed by any change at Westminster.
Balfour duly established these committees before his government fell and Esher was appointed a permanent member. He
refused Balfour's offer of a G.C.B. lest it should be thought
that he was a 'spy' left behind by Balfour. When Haldane
became Secretary of State for War, as the King and Esher
had hoped, Esher noted that on the day of the appointment
he had a 'long and most satisfactory talk' with Haldane, who
'professes that he "is willing to be nobbled" by our Committee'. Esher then made several telephone calls that resulted
in the general of his own choice agreeing to become Haldane's
private secretary and to Haldane's agreeing to interview him.
'This means,' added Esher, 'that we shall arrange it. Of course
nothing could indicate more clearly the "nobbling" of Haldane
by our Committee.'[b]

The results were satisfactory to the King, who was informed
by Esher of every development. The Government changed and
speeches were made about peace, but the permanent committees
of the Defence Committee functioned in complete secrecy.
Campbell-Bannerman was not much interested and proved
amenable. Haldane was the effective link. On 19 December
1905 Esher wrote him a long and able letter about the nature
of the British Army, which, he pointed out, is officered by
volunteers who all come from the same 'caste, with caste
prejudices'. In May of the next year he further explained to the
King that the Army Committee

'was composed of a large majority of persons who hold
or have held commissions in your Majesty's *Regular* Army,
and whose prejudices may be reasonably assumed to be
favourable to the Regular, when brought into accidental
conflict of interests with the Auxiliary Forces.

With one exception, the Committee is composed of men

who by political conviction, birth, station, and education are opposed to the Government now in office, and whose predilections therefore may be assumed to be strongly in favour of maintaining the authority of the Crown over all armed forces, whether Regular or Auxiliary, and opposed absolutely to anything in the shape of what is generally understood by the term "Citizen Army".'[c]

It would be irrelevant here to follow the controversies over Haldane's army reforms and the Territorial Army. What is important to our purpose here is that the King was party, quite constitutionally, to a battle behind the scenes which only very occasionally burst into public knowledge. Esher was himself on one occasion an object of public attack during the fight over the Big Navy proposals. He was extremely annoyed. He personally saw to it that Repington, then military correspondent of *The Times*, was kept well informed, and he had full discussions with Northcliffe, and Kennedy Jones, then editor of the *Daily Mail*. Support for the new Territorial Army came also from a play by Guy du Maurier which was produced by James Barrie, a close friend of Lord Esher. The play was called *An Englishman's Home*; it 'presented dramatically the consequence of failure to prepare against the dangers of invasion'.[d]

Esher's own position was always clear. He remarked that what France needed was 'a successful war', though he was on occasion troubled lest Admiral Fisher should start a European war all by himself. He was the only man who dared to scold Fisher; he could do so because he was a close friend of the King. For that reason and none other, Fisher was persuaded reluctantly and with the worst possible grace to co-operate in some measure with the Committee of Defence.

Throughout this fascinating correspondence in which Esher informed and advised the King about every detail of defence policy, discussed who should succeed Campbell-Bannerman, how to manage personalities as difficult as Fisher and Kitchener —in all these secret matters the King welcomed Esher's advice. Neither of them had any respect for the House of Commons, where Churchill, ironically enough today, was the leading spirit in the demand for economy in the Service estimates.

We find Esher writing to Knollys—that is, to the King—informing him that Haldane 'alone stands between us and Churchill'. Haldane, he reported to the King, had told the Premier that he 'would under no pressure or inducement vacate the W.O. [War Office]' or agree to a single cut in the army establishment. 'He is a courageous man, but no man can stand up for ever, *if he is alone*, and I wish he could be strengthened by the feeling that in this desperate struggle he has the King's good wishes.' This request was the more necessary because Edward was strongly opposed to some of Haldane's proposals for the new Territorial Army. Indeed, the King had directly opposed Haldane's scheme and it was not, as we learn from Haldane's biographer, 'until the King returned from Biarritz and Haldane saw him personally that he was able to secure the withdrawal of his opposition'. He persuaded the King that he had been misled and wrote to his mother:

> 'I have just come from breakfasting with the King. We were quite alone in a small room. I had a most agreeable interview and everything is smooth now. I explained to him about the Territorial Artillery. He quite understands. He is as keen as ever about the Territorial Army and agreed to my suggestion that the battalions have colours, and he told me that he would like to give as many as possible of these himself, when the time came. We had a very simple breakfast, not so good as at home.'e

Lloyd George was Churchill's partner in his fight against the Committee of Defence and when he asked Esher to give evidence before a government committee to enquire into the question of economy, Esher refused on the ground that he was an expert on policy, not finance. At that time Lloyd George, who had been a pro-Boer and was the white hope of all radicals, was regarded by the Establishment as a most dangerous character. Here again, the King's influence was sought.

Esher told the King that he did not believe in his heart Lloyd George cared a bit for economy and that he would be quite 'ready to face Parliament with any amount of deficit, and to "go" for a big Navy'. The problem for both Winston and Lloyd George, he said, was to 'find a bridge' which would satisfy their *amour propre*. A few weeks later Esher noted in his diary that: 'The King sent for Ll. George at my suggestion and this evening he sent for me. He was in one of his most charming moods. . . . He liked Ll. George and is not much frightened by what the latter told him of his budget. . . .'

Esher and the King were both right. Esher noted in 1910 that the imperialist wing of the Cabinet—in this case represented by Grey and Crewe—agreed that 'Winston Churchill has shown marked improvement during the elections, in grasp and tone. They both say, "the other one" [Lloyd George] is incorrigible. *Nous Verrons!* Twenty years ago, much the same could have been said of Chamberlain.' Only six years later Lloyd George was leading the wartime Coalition with the Tories and driving his old Radical supporters to despair.

In 1910, however, Esher and Edward VII were premature in deciding that Lloyd George was not dangerous. His struggle with the Committee of Imperial Defence and above all with Sir Douglas Haig, whom George V privately and strenuously supported throughout the war, was a set battle between the Establishment and a still recalcitrant Premier.

Haig's career, as Captain Liddell Hart had recently made clear, was from the first largely built on royal favour.[f] He failed in the entrance examination to the Staff College because of a weakness in mathematics, combined with colour blindness. Three years later he was nevertheless accepted and the qualifying examination excused. 'He owed this special favour,' says Liddell Hart, 'to royal influence.' The favourable impression he made at the Staff College was no doubt deepened 'by the frequency with which he attended shooting parties given by his elder sister, Henrietta, for the Prince of Wales'. In 1898, when serving on the Staff in the Sudan, he was encouraged to continue a private correspondence with the Prince of Wales; as always, he bitterly criticized his superior officers. This correspondence continued when the Prince of Wales had become Edward VII and Haig was Inspector-General of Cavalry in India. The correspondence became frankly political and dealt with the famous controversy between Curzon, the Viceroy, and Kitchener, Commander-in-Chief. Haig claimed that the decision of policy was largely due to 'the King's influence, following the line of his own advice'. While on leave and staying at Buckingham Palace, Haig married one of the Queen's maids of honour. The King wanted Haig back in England at the War Office; how this was eventually brought about in 1905 may be read in Esher's papers. When the war came he was Commander-in-Chief at Aldershot and in a position to exploit fully his friendship with George V.

To understand the struggle that followed we must remember that when war broke out in 1914 the loyalty of the Army to the Liberal Government in power was at breaking point, as a result of the Ulster dispute. The High Command began the war with the fixed idea that it would be won by the direct assault of millions of British and French soldiers against the massed German armies, the first of whose onrush had taken them through Belgium into France. The appalling casualty lists at Loos, Ypres, Vimy, the Somme, Cambrai and Passchendaele are the background of this struggle.

The more live-minded politicians, including Lloyd George and Churchill, were horrified by the loss of life and enraged by the refusal of Haig, Sir William Robertson and the French general staff to look for any less costly and more rewarding alternative. In October 1915 Robertson was warning Haig of the danger 'of our being dragged into a big campaign in the Balkans', and urging him to mobilize his friends in the Government against any change of strategy. Haig said he disliked intriguing in such a way, but would explain their views to the King, with whom he was dining that night. If Robertson became C.I.G.S., as he hoped, he would make the Government stick to a sound policy. Robertson remarked: 'We could win so easily if we acted rightly.'[g]

To maintain the policy of attrition on the Western front

which was to win the war so easily, it seemed necessary to keep Asquith in office and Churchill out of harm's way. Churchill's imaginative, but ill-managed, attempt to penetrate the Continent through Gallipoli had been a disastrous failure; it confirmed the set views of the General Staff and conditioned the British public in favour of a purely Western strategy. All efforts to break the pattern of slaughter in the West by a diversionary attack in Eastern Europe were treated by the soldiers as wild civilian romanticism. It was round this issue that the struggle for power turned. After the war Lloyd George wrote: 'We were about to witness a very determined effort not the first nor the last—made by this party to form a cabal which would overthrow the existing war cabinet and especially its Chief, and enthrone a government which would be practically the nominee and menial of this military party.' Robertson, and behind him Haig, were the centre of this military group. They assumed that sooner or later they must break through by sheer weight of metal and men, and they believed, against all the evidence, in their own unique competence. Lloyd George, on his side, fought with cunning and even duplicity. He went to the length of making a private arrangement with Nivelle, the new French Commander-in-Chief, to put Haig under his control. He did not inform Haig or Robertson, so that they found themselves trapped at a conference in Calais with no alternative to accepting the Premier's plan, at least for the coming offensive. Haig at once wrote in full to the King and was received by him a few weeks later at Buckingham Palace. Haig made this note in his private papers:

> 'The King . . . stated that he would "support me through thick and thin", but I must be careful not to resign, because Lloyd George would then appeal to the country for support and would probably come back with a great majority. . . . The King's position would then be very difficult. . . . We went over the whole Calais Conference. . . . The King said my account agreed entirely with Robertson's. He was furious with Lloyd George, and said he was to see him tomorrow.'[h]

Many books have dealt with one or other aspect of this extraordinary struggle. Lloyd George believed himself to be defending the cause of civil government against military dictatorship, and he was prepared to go to almost any length to win. In his memoirs he has described the lies that were put about by the generals and their journalist friends to support the theory of inevitable victory by attrition. British casualties were, as far as possible, minimized; German casualty figures deliberately multiplied. General Charteris, who managed these things for Haig, cannot be defended on the ground that this propaganda was necessary to keep up public morale; its main use was to deceive ministers and other politicians who might have insisted on a different policy if the truth had been known. All this has been fully exposed by Lloyd George and others, but until the publication of Haig's *Private Papers* and Beaverbrook's *Men and Power*, the part that the King played was not publicly known. When Lloyd George wrote he still hoped to return to the political stage, and in his bitter denunciation of Haig and his staff said nothing about the King's part in supporting Haig.

The quality above all others which Haig possessed and the King admired was his tenacity, his 'rocklike calm' in the face of the disasters his policy ensured. Lloyd George was, in their view, an ignorant Welsh mountebank. The Army was especially the King's province and a matter for experts. Politicians, the King said bluntly, must not interfere with strategy. He told Haig that he should always write to his Private Secretary and that no one else would know. Haig fully availed himself of the permission and made all the use he could of the King in his numerous intrigues. Lord Kitchener was drowned at sea, but Sir John French, whose complete incompetence as Commander-in-Chief was obvious after the first few months of the war, was only with difficulty removed. Haig arranged for the King to come to France to facilitate the dismissal of French and his own appointment to succeed him. The manœuvre was, for the moment, defeated by an accident; most embarrassingly the King was thrown and hurt by the mare which Haig personally lent him. But Haig records, after a visit to the King in April

1916, that it was the King himself who had insisted in peremptory terms on the dismissal of French. Haig and Robertson had won control.[i]

The main battle was fought over the body of Sir William Robertson, the C.I.G.S. and Haig's most powerful supporter. Lloyd George tried a variety of expedients to get rid of Robertson. One was to pack him off to Russia. Sir William consulted Lord Derby, Minister of War, who advised him to refuse to go. Derby reported this in a confidential letter to the King, explaining that Robertson and he, 'standing together can, I believe, prevent any wild-cat schemes; but alone I feel I should fail. Moreover there would be no buffer between Lloyd George and Haig, which is essential.'

In the complicated intrigues, which eventually led to the substitution of Sir William Robertson by Sir Henry Wilson, the C.I.G.S., many of the leading politicians and generals, as well as such journalists as Repington, Lord Northcliffe and Lord Beaverbrook, were involved. At every point the Prime Minister found himself baffled by the King's support of Haig and Robertson. The two protagonists, Lloyd George and Haig, were both acutely aware that the strain of these horrifying offensives was breaking down the morale of the Army, that there was a point beyond which neither the men at the front nor their friends and relatives at home would put up with the slaughter, and that the French Army was near mutiny. Though it was hushed up, part of it did, in fact, mutiny in 1917, after the Russian Revolution.

It is doubtful if the King ever understood this aspect of the war. As early as December 1914 Haig himself remarked, with some surprise, that the King was 'inclined to think that all our troops are by nature brave and is ignorant of all the efforts which commanders must make to keep up the "morale" of their men in war, and of all the training which is necessary in peace, in order to enable a company, for instance, to go forward as an organized unit in the face of almost certain death'.

As I read the story of this fight against the background of the mounting casualty lists, I see that the case for Haig and Robertson is that, having made up their minds on the war of attrition in the West, they believed that the one fatal error would be to vacillate and divide the strength of the Allies by military diversions. I am reminded of Bertrand Russell's famous declension: 'I am firm; you are obstinate; he is a pig-headed-fool.' It is not easy to say at what point firmness becomes obstinacy and obstinacy folly. An effective commentary can be found in the journals of that astute observer and adviser of the King, Lord Esher, who in the terrible year of 1916 was supporting Haig to the full and explaining that somehow or other the gigantic failure of the Somme was not, after all, a defeat—in spite of hundreds of thousands of casualties. Very gradually he began to see the point of Lloyd George's argument. During 1915, 1916 and 1917 the British and French had fought ghastly offensives in the Somme, Vimy and Passchendaele; the Germans had overwhelmed Serbia, Roumania, Russia and Italy.[j]

It was not until February 1918 that Lloyd George felt strong enough politically to side-track Sir William Robertson and to appoint Sir Henry Wilson as C.I.G.S. He had, by then, the full support of the Cabinet and he acted without the King's knowledge. Lord Derby, who, as Secretary of State for War, regarded himself as pledged to support the military junta and at the same time wanted to be loyal to the Prime Minister, wrote pathetic letters to the King and alternately resigned and withdrew his resignation. How the affair looked to the Palace remained unknown until, in 1956, Lord Beaverbrook published Lord Stamfordham's memoranda setting out the full facts.

Lloyd George finally made clear his determination to get rid of Robertson. Stamfordham wrote begging 'Sir William Robertson, in the King's name, not to relinquish his post as C.I.G.S.' How tough the King's resistance was is clear from the record of his meeting with Lloyd George on 16 February. Before he saw the King, Lloyd George told Stamfordham that 'the question of Sir William Robertson had now reached a point that if His Majesty insisted upon his (Sir W.R.) remaining in office on the terms he laid down, the Government could not carry on, and the King would have to find other Ministers. The Government *must* govern, whereas this was practically military dictation.' Stamfordham adds that he assured 'the Prime Minister that His Majesty had no idea of making such insistence'.

The King then saw the Prime Minister, who maintained his position. The King and Lord Derby submitted to what had now become a Cabinet decision. But, to Lloyd George's chagrin, Haig abandoned Robertson and remained Commander-in-Chief until the end of the war. In the end, by accepting Foch as Supreme Allied Commander, Lloyd George had at last had the satisfaction of subordinating Haig to someone, though not to himself.

This battle, which so terribly concerned the life of Britain, had throughout been fought behind the scenes between a democratically chosen Premier and a military junta, powerfully and secretly supported by the King. Lloyd George was at a grave disadvantage because all that passed between him and the King was secret; the King and his friends had also to be cautious because in the last resort Lloyd George could have thrown usage to the winds and appealed to the House of Commons and the electorate. Victory must be awarded to the Establishment, since the policy of attrition—which finally succeeded only because the Americans came to the rescue— was continued to the very bitter end. In public the honours were shared between Lloyd George and Field Marshal Haig.

5

STRANGE INTERLUDE

'On ne Baldwine pas avec l'amour.'—*Le Canard enchaîné*

'Isn't is very dreadful that Edward VIII, son of our Beloved King George, should bring Hollywood ideals to Britain? Surely he could have found some sweet British Girl.'—Letter in *Daily Express*

'May I suggest that if we are to believe the teachings of our Church, the All Highest did not think it beneath His dignity to take unto Himself "a commoner" to wife, thereby giving us The Master—The King of Kings.'—Letter in *Daily Mirror*

'We all share the Archbishop's regret that Edward VIII insists on marrying the woman with whom he happened to fall in love.'—Letter in *Sunday Referee*

'Primed with instructions from Russia—to get rid of the King—Mr. Baldwin has had a busy week—backwards and forwards—backwards and forwards—several times a day to hold a pistol to the head of the King, crying, "Do my will—or—abdicate".'—Lady Houston in *Saturday Review*

'In times of crisis the vast majority of folks turn for comfort and enlightenment to one of the following—Religion—Music—Poetry. Discarding the former two, may we not turn to poetry for much needed guidance? Have you thought of approaching the Poet Laureate? It seems to me that if inspiration came to him he could produce six or eight lines which would result in presenting to all concerned the real picture in its proper focus, with the

proper settlement resulting.'—Mr. A. E. Lawson, former
Derbyshire county cricket captain, in the *Sunday Dispatch*

'*Many thousands of you who applied for our Coronation Tea Set
will be interested to know that we have now made arrangements
to supply this tea set to you in three alternative forms. Firstly:
with the picture of Edward VIII on the bread-and-butter plate, as
originally announced. Secondly: with a picture of King George
VI and Queen Elizabeth on the bread-and-butter plate. Thirdly:
for those readers who would like to have the tea set and bread-
and-butter plates bearing the picture of Edward VIII and King
George VI and Queen Elizabeth, we are prepared to supply the
tea set and both bread-and-butter plates for an extra 6d., making
your total remittance 5s., instead of 4s. 6d., as the amount to be
sent with the completed Order Form.'*—Woman's Illustrated*

'*Serious-minded King George VI has many qualities to endear
him to the people.

'He is a better boxer than was Edward VIII, plays a stronger
game of tennis—though he is left-handed with the racquet—
enjoys grouse shooting, and has a mechanical bent.'*—News
Review*

'*We know no spectacle so ridiculous as the British public in one
of its periodical fits of morality. In general, elopements, divorces,
and family quarrels pass with little notice. We read the scandal,
talk about it for a day, and forget it. But once in six or seven
years our virtue becomes outrageous. We cannot suffer the laws
of religion and decency to be violated. We must make a stand
against vice. We must teach libertines that the English people
appreciate the importance of domestic ties. Accordingly some
unfortunate man, in no respect more depraved than hundreds
whose offences have been treated with lenity, is singled out as
an expiatory sacrifice. If he has children, they are to be taken
from him. He is cut by the higher orders, and hissed by the lower.
He is, in truth, a sort of whipping-boy, by whose vicarious agonies
all the other transgressors of the same class are, it is supposed,
sufficiently chastised. We reflect very complacently on our own
severity, and compare with great pride the high standard of*

*morals established in England with the Parisian laxity. At length
our anger is satiated. Our victim is ruined and heartbroken.
And our virtue goes quietly to sleep for seven years more.'*—
Macaulay's *Essay on Byron*, 1831

THE story of Edward VIII's brief reign makes a strange interlude in the history of British Monarchy. Its significance was
not constitutional. He behaved, indeed, with the strictest
constitutional propriety and ran no risk of damaging the
throne by permitting the formation of a King's Party. He
abdicated because he could not fulfil the domestic image of
British Monarchy which had been established by his grand-
mother and his father. It is interesting now to speculate
whether, if he had been stronger and more purposeful, he
could have re-shaped the pattern of monarchy in this country.
He could not be a father-figure, but could he, within the limits
imposed upon him, have created a more personal and more
democratic type of king, symbolizing the arrival of a new and
less conventional generation?

Some saw him as a champion of youth and modern ideas.
He did not disguise his distaste for much of the expected ritual of
royalty. His speeches were freshly worded and seemed sometimes
to have been written by himself. It was no accident that in his
abdication announcement he omitted to call himself 'King by
the Grace of God, Defender of the Faith'. He did not regard
himself as a Defender of the Faith. His father used such phrases
and spoke of God's care of his people and his Commonwealth
with simplicity and sincerity. King George's Christmas broad-
casts, greatly appreciated by his subjects, revealed the same
unthinking acceptance of the eternal truths of the Anglican
creed that characterized the utterances of his grandmother.
But Edward VIII was in revolt against the past; the fear that
unorthodox opinions and an unconventional private life might
mar the success of his reign was already apparent in the un-
easy balance of adulation and admonition achieved in the
accession speeches of the Prime Minister and the Archbishop
of Canterbury.

The King was in fact unconventional, but not, as some

people imagined, any kind of socialist. He disturbed Conservatives by contributing to the miners' relief fund during the 1926 strike and he did not disguise his view that society could be improved. He also wondered why a king should not be allowed to walk in the streets, wear a bowler-hat and carry an umbrella. He did not agree with Sir Frederick Ponsonby, his father's Keeper of the Privy Purse, who told him, while still Prince of Wales, that he ran the risk of making himself too accessible. 'The Monarchy,' said Sir Frederick, 'must always retain an element of mystery. A prince should not show himself too much. The Monarchy must remain on a pedestal.' The Prince differed, but Ponsonby, echoing a famous passage from Walter Bagehot, replied: 'If you bring it down to the people, the Crown will lose its mystery and its influence.' 'I do not agree,' said the Prince; 'times are changing.' But Ponsonby replied: 'I am older than you, sir. I have been with your father, your grandfather and your great-grandmother. They all understood; you are quite mistaken.'

Was he mistaken? It was true that no monarch since George III—and he was insane at the time—had walked unattended among common people in the streets. Some thought that Edward VIII had taken the first steps towards the Scandinavian monarchy, where royal personages may be rung on the telephone and have been seen riding bicycles. Edward had no liking for bicycles, but he complained that he need not always use the Daimler.

The weakness of Edward was that he was not sure what he wanted to do. He writes of himself in his younger days: 'Given my character, my roving curiosity and independence, my life appeared to form a disconnected pattern—duty without decision, service without responsibility, pomp without power.' In fact, he took his kingly duties extremely seriously and it is a common error to think that he chose, in the cant phrase, 'love rather than duty'. He knew that he could not perform his duties without being with the woman he loved and he thought it his duty to abdicate rather than to do without her. His fatal error in negotiating with Baldwin was to ask the Prime Minister to consult the Dominions; by submitting the issue of morganatic marriage as a matter of constitutional advice, he played into the hands of Baldwin and the Archbishop. For 'advice', in its technical context, means the instruction given by the Prime Minister which the King has to obey. Baldwin had only to reply that the Cabinet and the Dominion governments were opposed to the suggestion and the issue was closed.

Edward could have behaved like his forefathers; no one, certainly not the Prime Minister, would have complained, as he says, about a discreet affair, a side door with a latchkey and an illicit relationship with Mrs. Simpson. But if he was determined to marry, abdication was the only way—unless he was prepared to flout the Constitution. A King's Party was growing up; he might have challenged the authority of the Cabinet. But he was loyal to his oath as constitutional monarch. He had no thought of refusing the advice of the Premier, even when Mr. Churchill painted a rosy view of his future as a new kind of king with Mr. Baldwin humiliated at his feet; even when Lord Beaverbrook came rushing back from America to give his support; even when M.P.s championed his cause in the House; least of all when the Fascists, led by Sir Oswald Mosley, began organizing squads of toughs in the streets and Communists began demonstrating in his favour. He 'put out of mind all thoughts of challenging the Prime Minister . . . by making a stand for myself I should have left the scars of a civil war. A civil war is the worst of all wars. Its passions soar highest, its hatreds last longest. And a civil war is not less a war when it is fought in words and not in blood.' He saw that to fight such a battle would permanently damage the Monarchy and that he refused to do.

One other course was open to Edward which neither he nor anyone else at that time appears to have considered. Here was the unique opportunity for translating into reality Bernard Shaw's fantasy in *The Apple Cart*. If King Edward had abdicated, married as he wished and refused a dukedom, what could have prevented him from entering politics as a private citizen? Like King Magnus in Shaw's play, he could have offered himself as candidate for the borough of Windsor or, indeed, for any other borough. He would certainly have been a popular candidate.

As it was, the 'King's Party' came to nothing for lack of a king willing to accept its support. When Winston Churchill finally attempted in the House of Commons to obtain a delay which would benefit the King's case, he was, in effect, howled down. The King had put himself into the position from which there was no constitutional alternative to abdication. Therefore, puritanism was once again, as in the seventeenth century, associated with parliamentarianism. People who were least inclined to take a puritanical view of the King's way of life were compelled to support the Archbishop and the Prime Minister in the interests of Parliamentary government. Those who were least puritanical and most hostile to the Prime Minister were compelled to behave like Roundheads. They detested what they regarded as a hypocritical conspiracy engineered by the Prime Minister, the editor of *The Times* and the Archbishop of Canterbury. But if the alternative was an alliance with a twentieth-century royalist party, they had to choose to be Parliamentarians. The King went across the water without leaving a Cavalier party behind him and victory went by default to the Parliamentarians and puritans.

A later generation has forgotten the shock of the King's abdication. A moment had come when the failings of the ruling King were publicly admitted. I recalled, as we left a cinema on the night of 2 December 1936, discussing with a friend the 'scandal' round the throne and the possibility that it might lead to the King's abdication. 'Hush, sir, hush,' said a deeply shocked voice behind me. Colonel Blimp had not yet discovered that the monarchical taboo was shattered. He was still manfully trying to impose silence, even though all the world's press, except the British, had long been making headlines out of Edward and Mrs. Simpson. In England the story had long been the most popular topic of discussion in clubs and round the dining tables of journalists and top people. The American dailies, thriving on gossip about the British throne, had no general circulation in England: British wholesalers cut out references to the Monarchy (even at the sacrifice of whole pages) before they allowed magazines like *Time* to appear on English bookstalls. Only those who subscribed directly to American papers or who received cuttings from American friends knew how widely the scandal had spread on the other side of the Atlantic. The well informed might nudge one another when they saw Mrs. Simpson's name in the Court Circular or noted her attractive figure in photographs of the guests at Fort Belvedere or on the royal yacht. But such indirect references to the best of all news stories were all the British press allowed itself.

It was widely assumed, especially in the United States, that the British press was subject to a highly competent form of censorship. Lord Beaverbrook has made clear his own part in persuading Fleet Street to keep silent. But Lord Beaverbrook and Lord Rothermere had no influence on the *Daily Worker* or *The Times* or the independent weekly reviews. Yet they too sacrificed sales by a unique reticence. The truth is that no newspaper would have thought it good policy to win a temporary circulation boost by printing scandal about the royal family. Even the Simpson divorce case, which was news no one could be blamed for printing, was 'played down'. Certainly telephone calls between Fleet Street, Whitehall and Buckingham Palace played their part. But the absence of any kind of comment even in weekly reviews and papers which were not members of the Newspaper Press Association was due to other causes. One inhibiting factor was the law of libel; any comment would have been guarded and evasive. Far more important, however, was the royal taboo which everyone concerned with a newspaper, from the proprietor and editor to the reporters and compositors, found it immensely difficult to break.

It may be of interest for me to give my own experience. As editor of an independent weekly review, I naturally knew about the headlines in the foreign press, and debated what comment I should make. I agreed with a friend of the King who urged that it would be disgraceful to start a scandal in England about what was after all a matter which concerned the King only. He was happy for the first time in his life; why interfere? But the situation changed when I was told authoritatively and confidentially that the King had made up his mind to marry Mrs.

Simpson. I was also told that he would be pleased if a serious discussion of the constitutional issue began in a responsible and sympathetic paper such as the one I edited. If the story broke in this way the scandalous headlines in the popular press would be forestalled, and possibly the real issues would be discussed. This removed all doubts, since the choice of the Queen, or for that matter the King's wife, is indubitably a matter of public importance. So I wrote an article arguing that the King had as much right to marry the woman of his choice as anyone else, and that if there were good reasons against Mrs. Simpson as Queen, there would be none against a morganatic marriage. Since the information of the King's intention had come to me from him, I sent the article to him to see. It was returned with a message that he would be glad if I went ahead and published it. I was about to send it to the printer (with some misgivings about whether they would accept it) when I received a further message asking me to wait a week because its publication might damage the chances of a settlement. The King, in short, still had some hope of persuading Mr. Baldwin; an article in the *New Statesman* might be taken as a declaration of war or at least as a sign of an intention to appeal to public opinion against the Government. So I held up the article. Then came a blow with a Blunt instrument, as jesters said at the time, and my article died a natural death.

During the week before the news actually broke, all Fleet Street was aware that the King's attachment to Mrs. Simpson could not be much longer concealed. It had to cope with an immense shock to a public complacency that it had itself done much to foster. The Monarchy was not, after all, perfect, and proprietors and editors were obviously flummoxed by not knowing how the public would take the news. There was rich comedy in their efforts to have it both ways. How be loyal and sustain the national myth while exploiting a wonderful news story? How appear to give a lead when they did not know in which direction public sentiment would move? They were constantly forced to reiterate that the King was 'after all human'. People had to be let into the secret that the Monarchy was not perfect, because otherwise the situation was inexplicable.

On 2 December Bishop Blunt's apparently innocent refer-
ence to the King's failure to appreciate God's grace was the
signal for which all the newspapers had been waiting. Their
material was ready; their comments were not. On the first day
they reported the Bishop's statement without editorial comment.
In strict privacy editors had been writing and rewriting innumerable leading articles; one, I was told, wrote seventeen.
The Times from the beginning showed inside knowledge; even
before the crisis it began to 'write up' the Duke and Duchess of
York. The *Telegraph* was also from the outset clearly for Mr.
Baldwin. It argued that the King would certainly choose duty
even at the expense of personal happiness, but made it clear
that it preferred abdication if he made the wrong choice.[a]

The issue abruptly changed when Mr. Baldwin stated that
the King had asked for special legislation to enable him to
make a morganatic marriage and that the Cabinet, after
consulting the Dominion governments and the Opposition
leaders, had refused. From that time onwards the only supporters of the marriage were those who were prepared to risk a
revival of the seventeenth-century struggle between Crown and
Parliament. Hitherto the division had been between those who
held, either for reasons of religion or snobbery, that the
marriage was unsuitable and those who were untroubled by the
prospect of the King marrying a commoner, an American and
a divorcee. It now became a simple issue of the King's right to
act against the Prime Minister's 'advice'. The *Catholic Times*
declared that the crisis was a ramp, contrived by the financiers.
The *Daily Worker* took much the same line, reporting Mr.
Harry Pollitt who spoke of the 'flummery and flapdoodle' of
the crisis. The apostles of Social Credit revived, in more
flamboyant forms than hitherto, Hilaire Belloc's thesis that the
King in our day should assume his sixteenth-century powers
in order to champion the cause of the people against twentieth-
century robber barons. In *Reynolds* Mr. Brailsford quietly
remarked that 'while England chatters about a lady from
Baltimore, Germany marches forward to the conquest of
Spain'.

The King, as we have seen, gave no countenance to the

motley army which rallied to his standard. Enquiries at the time led me to agree with a lobby correspondent who held that for about forty-eight hours there had been a real danger of the birth of a King's Party in the House as well as outside it, but even M.P.s who were personally inclined to oppose the Government on the morganatic issue were deterred by reports from their constituencies. Backing for the King's marriage seemed to be almost wholly confined to London. Scotland was firmly against. South Wales Members reported that the King's popularity was almost gone; the film of his recent visit was watched in cold silence in the very valleys where the same people had cheered him so vehemently only a few weeks before. Similar reports of solid opposition came from all parts of the country. The marriage just did not fit into the pattern expected of a British king. I enjoyed the comment of a foxhunting squire who was in the process of divorcing his wife; he held that 'the King was no gentleman'. Poor people in some parts of London were more tolerant. I talked to bus conductors, charwomen and workers. In the first days of the crisis the usual comment was that the King 'ought to marry anyone he likes, the same as anyone else'. A friend whose work brought her into contact with many poor people said that general opinion was summarized in a working woman's phrase: 'He's a naughty boy, but we don't want to lose him.' Another said: 'Of course he'd better marry her. It's no use living alongside someone you don't like. You only want to do them in.' But when the issue was clear and the news of the abdication was announced, a taxi-driver summed it up by saying regretfully: 'It wouldn't have done. It wouldn't have done.'

In this remarkable story the British press, wireless, public, Premier and House of Commons all behaved precisely according to pattern. On the night of King Edward's broadcast I heard the wireless announcer declare that the world stood amazed at the admirable behaviour of England in this unprecedented crisis. The phrase was part of a familiar tune. During the next few days it was repeated in one form or another in almost every British newspaper. We had behaved as always with astonishing sobriety, judgment, self-restraint.

Foreigners, it was implied, would have kicked over the traces in all sorts of unthinkable ways at the prospect of a royal abdication or a royal marriage with a woman who had appeared twice in the divorce courts.

This self-congratulation on our own modesty, reticence and other sterling gifts always marks British recovery from a shock. The crisis is resolved and the process of self-reassurance begins. The same pattern of behaviour was noticeable in the General Strike, in the economic crisis of 1931 and on various occasions when a financial scandal or example of personal corruption has been publicly exposed. On such occasions some of those things which the British ruling classes would not admit to be possible in this country have indubitably occurred. It is an axiom, resolutely upheld and only to be disputed by the contumacious, that, whilst other people have social divisions and revolutions, no class struggle exists in England. The General Strike, nevertheless, occurred. Similarly, bad finance and unsound economic policy might upset the economic stability of continental countries or of the United States; in England the banks were invulnerable and capitalism unshakable. Yet the economic crisis of 1931 occurred. Again, graft may be rampant abroad, but its absence is the peculiar glory of British public life. Yet City scandals do occur. In every case exactly the same technique is adopted. When the unprecedented had happened and could no longer be hidden, every effort was made to insist that it was an isolated incident having nothing to do with anything else in society, a mere aberration from the normal to which we could at once return when the incident was over. No reason to examine its causes or to consider whether the moral and social axioms that had been momentarily challenged were in need of revision. No reason to blame anybody, or to dwell on the past. No one so apt as Mr. Baldwin at saying the healing word. It was most needed in the abdication crisis. At first the confused public was like a man who had received a violent blow on the head and who feared in his pain and bewilderment that the injury might be permanent; it woke up a few days later in hospital to find Mr. Baldwin sitting by the bedside explaining that nothing very serious had really occurred, that the Monarchy was safer than ever and that it had proved the soundness of our Constitution that we were able to return to normal with another king, a family man like his father who would carry on the great traditions of British Monarchy and assure the stability of our future.

If matters could have remained there Mr. Baldwin would have pulled off a perfect job—a job as difficult and as successfully handled from his point of view as the General Strike. For complete success, however, he should have had the last word. His farewell to the King was a masterpiece; Edward alone knew its subtle dishonesty.[b]

The tone was perfect and would have been scarcely criticized had not the Archbishop of Canterbury caricatured it in a broadcast which nauseated a surprising number of people. Many will still recall Gerald Bullett's scathing quatrain on Cosmo Lang's broadcast. My version runs:

> My Lord Archbishop, what a scold you are!
> And when your man is down, how bold you are!
> Of charity how oddly scant you are!
> How Lang Oh Lord, How full of Cantuar![1]

This broadcast produced a remarkable outburst of anti-clerical feeling, not only in the weekly reviews, but in papers like the *Daily Telegraph*. Resentment against the Archbishop was not confined to intellectuals. The tone of his broadcast was judged to be that of a party leader who boasts of having done down his opponent—which is never a popular attitude in Britain. It contrasted altogether too sharply with the simplicity and directness of the Duke of Windsor's broadcast, in which everyone learnt that he had been prevented from speaking to the public by Mr. Baldwin and that he was abdicating for no other reason than that he wanted to marry a divorced woman.

There was little more criticism. A small group of left socialists polled five votes for a republican amendment. Mr. Maxton urged in eloquent but not inflammatory language

[1] An alternative version of the last line is: 'Old Lang swine, how full of Cantuar!'

T.C.A.T.E.—H

that monarchy was an out-of-date institution which naturally led to such crises in the twentieth century, and he was supported by four other members. One of whom, Mr. Buchanan, remarked, amid the eulogies of the departing King, that 'he had never heard so much humbug in his life'; if the eulogists believed what they said, 'why did they unload him?'. The Labour Party attitude, however, was expressed by Mr. Attlee, who said that socialists could not waste their time on abstract discussions about republicanism. Monarchy, it was true, had been absurdly played up in the past and invested with 'an unreal halo'. This had tended to obscure the realities.

What was the reality after the abdication? Mr. Maxton quoted Humpty Dumpty:

> All the King's Horses
> And all the King's men
> Could not put Humpty Dumpty
> Back again.

Shouts of 'together again' came from all parts of the House. Tension was relaxed. It was pleasant to correct the scansion of a misquoted nursery rhyme, but the correction did not dispose of Mr. Maxton's point, and the press at once set about putting Humpty Dumpty together again. Arrangements had already been made for a Council of Regency and the picture was quickly redrawn of the Monarchy restored in the image of George V. Impeccably, George VI, with his wife and daughters, sat on his father's throne. Everything that could be found to say about the new King was said; stress was laid on his work for boys' camps, on some remarks he had made about the need for social improvement, and above all about his happy and blameless family life. All the resources of propaganda were ready to build up the new King and Queen and to re-establish the approved pattern of British Monarchy.

6

TV MONARCHY

GEORGE VI was the rare example of a truly reluctant monarch. He had never been clever, was free from pretence and did not want publicity. His brother David had always been the bright boy of the family, destined for the throne with its problems, responsibilities and inevitable notoriety. George had looked forward to the quiet life of a country gentleman. He never wholly overcame his nervous stammer; the dread of standing before the public tongue-tied, as he had before his father, made his sudden elevation a formidable ordeal. That he was able to face it successfully was in large measure due to the support of his wife, who had just the social gifts that George lacked.

Temperamentally, however, George was well suited to the routine life now expected of him. He was a family man and as near as maybe a replica of George V. Like his father, he was a conventional Tory. I can make nothing of his biographer's remark that he was 'not pro-conservative or anti-socialist'. He was constantly and frankly both. Sir John Wheeler-Bennett must mean that he did not allow his prejudices to interfere with his constitutional duty; that he behaved in a friendly and courteous way towards Labour ministers and that when they had both overcome the initial shyness, he and Attlee got on well together. In private he even read socialist literature. Like Edward VII when he met Lloyd George, George VI was relieved to find that Aneurin Bevan was not a devil, but, on the contrary, charming and 'easy to talk to'. The King was especially interested in the new Minister's housing programme. He was genuinely concerned to improve working-class conditions. But his fear of change was scarcely less than his father's had been. He frequently warned Attlee about the perilous speed at which he thought the Labour Government was proceeding and wrote repeating Tory allegations that the liberty of the subject was imperilled by its policy. Attlee behaved just as Liberal ministers had done in the past when they had to overcome the Monarch's conservative hesitations. He was always respectful and ready, in the midst of an over-burdened life, to write long explanations of his policy. He had a high regard for the King and after his death spoke warmly about his democratic readiness to accept social change.

Where George VI proved most exacting was over the question of Indian independence. He stuck stoutly to the view that 'India must be governed'. He had been horrified to learn from Mr. Churchill as early as July 1942 that all three parties in the House were 'quite prepared to give up India after the war'. He bitterly opposed Lord Wavell's proposal, when he was appointed Viceroy, 'to release Gandhi and Nehru from prison and to invite them to become members of the Viceroy's Council'. In his diary he wrote that 'Gandhi is now discredited in U.S.A. and in India and to let him out of confinement now is suicidal policy'.[b] Here, as always, he instinctively echoed a true-blue point of view, but was, of course, prepared in the end to accept advice which constitutionally he could not reject. Historically, the importance of his reign is that he restored the ideal conception of the domestically correct and conventional monarch which for the moment had been shattered by his brother's abdication. In so doing he laid the foundation on which the new TV Monarchy was built.

The trumpetings and hurrahs that heralded the accession of the young and attractive Queen and her handsome and intelligent consort have never in this country been surpassed in noise and splendour. No one can say that the press and public failed in loyalty, respect or flattery. Everyone enjoyed the first TV coronation; it was a superb spectacle. If there was some reaction afterwards that was because the claims made for the Monarchy and the significance read into the ceremony was extravagant. There is a wide gap between enjoying a national holiday on which a popular young Queen is crowned and sharing in a 'national communion service' which, in the

'Morning After', by David Low

Archbishop's words, is to bring the whole country close to the Kingdom of Heaven.

To suggest that the elaborate symbolism of the ceremony was understood by the mass of viewers is, I suppose, the type of mysticism which one must forgive in an archbishop. A moment's reflection exposes its unreality. The coronation was an Anglican service, and only a few of those who enjoyed it were members of the Church of England. None but the erudite could be expected to gather spiritual benefit from its obscure excursions into the legendary past. Perhaps more would have appreciated the historic significance of the coronation oath, in which the Queen swore to serve her people, if this simple and intelligible promise had not been lost in a mysterious jargon which delights specialists in heraldry and ecclesiastical tradition.

Reaction came speedily. The first sign was a cartoon by David Low in the *Manchester Guardian* which showed the dishevelled British public waking up to face the bill the morning after.[1] This was indeed to bring the sublime down to earth with a bump. Letters of angry protest poured into the *Guardian*, which, rather oddly, apologized for having told the truth too soon, before the public was ready to listen. An equal spate of letters followed in support of David Low; many of them seemed to come from old-fashioned radicals who objected to so lavish an expenditure of public money and so unrestrained an outpouring of sycophantic sentiment. There was also, it seemed, a business side to the matter. The coronation had been very good for retail trade and there had been large withdrawals from national savings.

[1] The Financial Secretary to the Treasury on March 10th 1952 stated that in addition to the £925,000 voted for the coronation in the Civil Estimates 'rather more than £1,000,000 would fall on ordinary votes in connection with the Coronation'. A few were rude enough to point out that Mr. R. A. Butler, the Chancellor of the Exchequer, had spoken only a few days before of the need of financial stringency and of the economic peril involved in the wage demands of shop-assistants, railwaymen and miners. Some Labour Members recalled that the Conservatives had objected to the expenses of the Festival of Britain the year before (when Labour was in office) and argued that the Conservatives were boosting the coronation for electoral reasons.

It is an error to assume that all classes are similarly affected by the cult of royalty. An American resident in this country had written soon after the abdication that: 'Anyone who has lived in England knows that Royalty is the special toy of the upper middle class. The so-called "lower classes" may reveal genuine enthusiasm at a coronation or jubilee of their king, but royalty plays no part in their lives. To the middle class, on the other hand, the monarchy with its titles, distinctions and exclusiveness is the very basis of their social life. The British middle-class Babbitt, by identifying himself and his family with Royalty, in some mysterious manner partakes of the virtue of Royalty which is aloofness from the mass of ordinary humanity.'c Ten years later Mr. Richard Hoggart, a perceptive analyst of social England, made the same point with less vehemence. The working classes do not speak in terms of worship or adulation such as some newspapers and biographers assume to be necessary when referring to royal personages. The working classes, he writes:

'are not royalists by principle. Nor do most harbour resentment against it; they have little heat. They either ignore it or, if they are interested, the interest is for what can be translated into the personal. Since they are "personalists" and dramatists, they are more interested in a few individual members of the Royal Family than in the less colourful figures of parliamentary government. I am not thinking of the period, usually in adolescence, when some girls find a glamour in the Royal Family similar to that they find in film stars; nor of the fervours of London crowds on special occasions. I am thinking chiefly of provincial working class women over twenty-five. Their menfolk are either quite uninterested in Royalty or vaguely hostile, since it tends to suggest to them the world of special parades in the Services, of "blanco and bullshit".'d

Anyone who has listened to the remarks made in the crowd at any of the great royal ceremonies, marriages, funerals or coronations, will have noticed a tone of easy familiarity and often of good-humoured ridicule. Primarily, mothers and fathers bring their children for the pageantry and the day's fun. Our industrial society is starved of fiestas. Coronations and royal marriages in Westminster Abbey are magnificent aesthetic spectacles. They have a religious setting, but to most people they are holidays, beanos, jollifications on an immense scale. What can be more memorable than a coach journey to London from a Lancashire town or Lincolnshire village, with the usual restraint thrown aside, a night perhaps spent sleeping in the Mall and a morning glimpse of a fairy princess in a glass coach? The reported comments do not suggest 'dedication'; they tend to deal with the cost of the robes ('She didn't buy that out of the housekeeping money'); with speculation about whether the Queen was over-burdened or enjoying herself, with comments on her choice of millinery, interspersed with arguments about whether her children were being well brought up and exclamations about the beauty of the prancing horses. This is all perfectly consistent with clubbing together to hang flags and bunting in the streets, organizing village sports and painting everything red, white and blue—from the flag-poles on the golf links to the tails of rabbits and fantail pigeons. 'It makes a bit of colour doesn't it?'e

Not every parish hung out bunting. The working-class Council of Stepney decided not to spend money on decorations but, instead, to send nearly a thousand children to the seaside for a fortnight's holiday and to present every old person with 'a gift parcel and a half-pound of tea in a souvenir caddy'. When it came to watching on TV, many sophisticated people, who were happy to cheer the Queen, were shocked to find that her coronation was wholly feudal. They had been told that the Monarchy symbolized our increasingly democratic way of life; but they watched a beautifully produced theatrical performance in which almost no one below the rank of a baron took part. (Was not the Moderator, dressed in black, the only exception?) Apart from the Queen herself, the chief roles were played by the Archbishop, the Earl Marshal and other persons with strangely medieval titles. Why, it was asked, if the object was to unite the nation, take the aristocracy out of mothballs (not even leavening it from the House of Commons) and then tell us that we were watching something that represented Britain and the Commonwealth? Real symbolism seems to have been missed. Working-class England would seem to have been forgotten, and so were the great majority of the Queen's subjects, who are not Christians, but non-believers, Buddhists, Hindus, Moslems or Africans who worship quite other gods. The Queen of Tonga's popularity should at least have given a hint. But no. Nothing was done to suggest that Elizabeth II is not only Queen of England. Even Scotland, where she is Elizabeth I, was left with a grievance. After months of steady B.B.C. and press publicity about the new Elizabethan Age, in which the second Elizabeth was to unify her subjects at home and throughout the world, the ceremony was more purely national, more aristocratic, more exclusive, more Anglican, more medieval, than ever before.

It was not the Queen's fault if she could not fulfil the role which her advisers and publicity officers were determined to present as hers. No one could complain that she did not work hard. The record of her activity is impressive. Mr. Morrah gives an alarming list of her duties. He describes her efforts to meet as many of her subjects at home and abroad as is humanly possible. If to 'meet' means to be 'seen by', then it is true that television and air travel have made it far more possible than ever before for the Queen to perform this function. Domestically, she has a busy life; she has her duties as a mother, must spend part of every day with her children and superintend the activities of her household. (Mr. Morrah does not pretend that she baths the baby or cooks the meals.) Then every day, and wherever she goes in this country, she is under an obligation to 'do her boxes' (King George V's phrase), which means that she must look at the telegrams and summaries of events which daily arrive for her in red dispatch boxes from her ministers in this country and Commonwealth nations. She follows current events and, says Mr. Morrah, has a retentive memory which enables her to take 'a rather malicious pleasure in catching out her staff on matters relating to the day's news'. She has personally to deal with selected letters from the immense correspondence that reaches the Palace every day. She replies to some of them, occasionally in her own hand. She must constantly be an 'artist's model'; her subjects demand that she seldom appear in the same dress, and she has often to sit for painters and photographers. A surprising amount of her time is taken in receiving foreign ambassadors and afterwards giving lunch to their wives and other important foreigners. She gives interviews to all those who represent her abroad, coming and going. She gains in this way a large store of knowledge and is able, as a result of talking to foreign ambassadors, to discuss with knowledge the countries to which her own ambassadors are going. She has also a full programme of official lunches and dinners and, as a new departure, has begun to entertain persons of interest and distinction from various walks of life at informal lunches in which, it seems, the traditional Palace protocol that in the royal presence one does not speak until one is spoken to, is not strictly observed.

The only comment that seems necessary on these aspects of the Queen's duties is that a visitor from America, for instance, may not see in this picture any great distinction from what goes on in the White House. He may, however, add that the historic prestige of monarchy makes entertainment in the Palace peculiarly impressive and indeed romantic. Whether a foreign guest comes away from entertainment in the Palace complaining of the antiquated formality of royal reception or waxing enthusiastic about its combined glamour and simplicity, depends no doubt partly on temperament and partly on whether he comes from Washington, Australia, Ghana or Moscow.

Another group of the Queen's duties includes most carefully prepared and skilfully managed tours of different parts of England. We learn with something akin to awe how precisely timed and minutely organized such tours must be. During a visit to Winchester, for instance, in order to keep her tight schedule and avoid causing disappointment, exactly so many minutes had to be allotted to meeting the mayor and other civic dignitaries, to showing herself to the crowd, to visiting the ancient public school and the famous cathedral and to reviewing the troops stationed there. All this has to be precisely timed; occasional minutes had to be found for her to transact some public business with the Premier, who happened to be in Winchester, and for Prince Philip to change from a lounge suit into uniform and back again. The whole programme had taken about eight and a half exhausting hours and throughout the day it was essential that never for a minute she should lose her 'air of freshness and vitality'.[f]

To all this must be added the public occasions when she must dress in her robes as Queen. The traditional ceremony in which she opens Parliament still has a well-understood significance; the extraordinary and antiquated snobbery of the Order of the Garter, performed at Windsor, seems no longer relevant to modern life. Comparatively few people today are interested in the fact that this order was founded by Edward III to commemorate 'the legendary glories of King Arthur's Round Table'.

Apart, of course, from these and other lesser occasions when the Queen has to dress up and show herself in her majesty, she has a large number of constitutional duties. She receives, usually weekly, visits from the Prime Minister, who explains to her, no doubt in less cumbersome detail than Mr. Gladstone used in reporting to Queen Victoria, the policy, activities and difficulties of her government; she also receives the Foreign Secretary and other ministers, if occasion demands it. The royal assent is necessary for every Act of Parliament; she does not append her personal signature, but authorizes a Commission to do this for her. Mr. Morrah finds an ingenious reason for holding that the formality of royal assent has value. He suggests, for example, that an occasion might arise when, owing to a sudden switch of the foreign kaleidoscope, a Bill authorizing the supply of nuclear weapons to a country which has joined a hostile alliance has passed the Lords and awaits the royal assent. In such a case, he remarks, 'no one would then be likely to attack the government' if Parliament learns that the royal assent has been withheld. This is probably true, but in these circumstances everyone would know in a monarchy, as in a republic, that it was the Prime Minister and not the

Head of State who had temporarily departed from constitutional usage.

In spite of the Queen's dutiful fulfilment of this exacting programme, she has been subjected to much open criticism and the Monarchy has suffered a series of psychological misfortunes. The basis of complaint has not been personal, though it has sometimes been expressed in unnecessarily wounding terms. She has been universally recognized as a good woman; in many respects she reminds us of the young Queen Victoria— though it must be added that her passion for racing would not have been approved by her great-grandmother. At first much criticism was directed at her limitations as a public speaker. The critics emphasized that this was apparently the result of inadequate tuition—not that this defence appeased outraged loyalists.

The basis for complaint has, however, not been personal at all. Many people of different classes and persuasions—not only a bunch of disgruntled intellectuals—have been nauseated by the sycophancy and ballyhoo of royal propaganda. Thoughtful people have also been disappointed by the failure of the young Queen and the Prince Consort to rejuvenate the court and discard the stiff protocol with which it is traditionally surrounded.

It seemed not unreasonable to hope that the long list of sinecures would be reduced and the pompous and archaic retinue of courtiers be replaced by a smaller number of persons who could build more normal contacts between the Queen and her subjects. The first bows to modernity were not impressive. The débutante receptions, which had become a subject of common ridicule, were abolished. 'Innocent parties' to divorce cases were allowed to enter the Royal Enclosure at Ascot. This concession was, however, nullified by the creation of the 'Queen's Lawn', which was even more exclusive. As for the 'Queen's Household', *Whitaker's Almanack* for 1961 includes almost nine columns, closely packed with names under this heading. After listing the well-known offices—the Lord Chamberlain, Lord Steward, Master of the Horse, Treasurer and Controller of the Household, Gold Sticks, A.D.C.s,

Mistress of the Robes, Ladies of the Bedchamber, Women and Extra Women of the Bedchamber, we come to the Private Secretary's office and staff, the Queen's Archives, Privy Purse and Treasurer, and the Royal Almonry—all with their staffs. Under the sub-heading of Lord Chamberlain's office there are Lords and Ladies in Waiting, Grooms in Waiting, Extra Grooms in Waiting, Gentlemen Ushers (ten), Extra Gentlemen Ushers (sixteen) as well as a Gentleman Usher to the Sword of State, Black Rod and Serjeants-at-arms. There is a separate office of Ascot and large Ecclesiastical and Medical Households. The Central Chancery of the Orders of Knighthood includes the Honourable Corps of Gentlemen-at-arms, the Queen's Bodyguard of the Yeomen of the Guard. The Master of the Household's Department has nine staff and the Royal Mews Department includes about forty Equerries and Extra Equerries. In addition there is the Scottish Household and the Queen's Bodyguard for Scotland as well as the Households of Prince Philip, the Queen Mother, the Duke of Gloucester and Princess Margaret. The total number of names is between 400 and 500.

More important has been the Crown's failure to build harmonious relations with the press. Reporters, chosen for duty at the Palace, declared that never before had it been so aloof and superior; Fleet Street was ribald about the snobbery of courtiers and public relations officers. These criticisms and resentments did not of course prevent the fullest exploitation of royal news-value; they merely resulted in an increasingly snide tone which crept almost imperceptibly into the fulsome accounts that daily appeared side by side with photographs of the Queen, the Duke, their children and all the members of the royal family. Articles and pictures in the most patriotic papers recorded the visits of the royal pair at the races, emphasizing that the Queen was animated and the Duke bored. Some even referred to their obvious divergence of tastes; one headline asked: 'What can the matter be?' Much was made of an incident in which the Queen and Duke failed to keep an expected rendezvous in Gibraltar. A bishop was interviewed about the Queen's addiction to racing; he suggested that she should ration her pleasures. It was undesirable that she should be too much associated with betting; she should set her subjects a good example. The most damaging adulation appeared in Sunday newspapers. Intimate accounts of the family upbringing by former servants of the royal household along with details of money spent on dress and entertainment are perhaps the speediest way to strip from monarchy the last vestiges of magic, of reverence and even of dignity.

It was not surprising that Commander Colville, who has been the chief press secretary at the Palace since 1947, should have sent a letter in January 1955 to the Press Council complaining that some employees of the royal household had broken the trust imposed on them. When entering the service of the Palace they are informed, as a condition of employment, that they may not 'give any person either verbally or in writing any information regarding Her Majesty or any member of the Royal Family which might be communicated to the press'.

In its annual report for 1956 the Press Council said it would be failing in candour if it pretended that the relations between Buckingham Palace and the press were happy and harmonious. This was putting things mildly in the year after the affair of Group Captain Townsend. In the following May Commander Colville had one of several private meetings with the Council. Speaking on ITV (18 June) Sir Gerald Barry criticized the Palace officials, saying that it was a standing complaint in Fleet Street that the people in Buckingham Palace are 'reluctant and standoffish and uncommunicative'. The *News Chronicle* volunteered some examples in the following year. It had learnt the dates of the coming royal visit to Canada and Australia before the official announcement. Commander Colville, asked to confirm the information, said he had 'no knowledge' of it. Again, when the Queen broke her holiday because of Sir Anthony Eden's resignation, the Palace pretended that she had come to London to do some shopping.

The Press Council, confronted with the press desire to learn all they could about the royal family, on the one hand, and, on the other, with the press treatment of Princess Margaret's reported courtship of Group Captain Townsend ('Come on,

Margaret, please make up your mind' and 'For Pete's sake, put him out of his misery') was obviously embarrassed. It divided the blame, saying that the Palace should provide a better news service, while the newspapers should not bribe Palace servants to reveal royal secrets and should handle royal news with discretion. Commander Colville accompanied the Queen and the Duke on their Canadian and American tour and was severely criticized in both countries. In Washington he was asked whether he would not change his attitude to the press after seeing the way in which Mr. Hagerty managed the President's publicity. He replied: 'Certainly not.' And in February 1960 he was quoted as saying that 'My job is for the most part to keep stories about the Queen out of the press.'

On one occasion Philip lost his temper with newspapermen and sprinkled water over those who came too close. Asked in Canada whether he would himself give a press conference, he said it would be no good because, unlike the American President, royalty had nothing to say about public policy; only two people would turn up! The newspapers reported, however, that he intended personally 'to review the dreary, starchy, so impersonal system of public and press contact that has some-how survived so long'. Prince Philip was himself reported as saying that he favoured a 'much more relaxed' attitude between the people and the royal family. Mr. Butler, a Canadian, was appointed assistant press officer to sweeten relations with the Commonwealth press. The Queen was criticized for visiting Portugal, the least democratic, if the 'oldest', of Britain's allies, and sending a deputy to celebrate Ghanaian independence. A later visit to Ghana was arranged which had to be cancelled because of the Queen's pregnancy. For once the Palace publicity was well advised. Dr. Nkrumah was early informed of the correct reason for the postponement of the trip and invited to England instead.

No one should quarrel, I think, with Commander Colville for endeavouring to stem the flood of much foolish, inaccurate and no doubt undesired publicity given to the royal family. When in January 1958 he told the Press Council that the Queen was distressed by press intrusion on her privacy, he no doubt had in mind newspaper interference with the education of Prince Charles and Princess Anne. It was also reported that at one time American magazines kept permanent correspondents in England with the job of prying into the private affairs of the royal family and that the police knew of as many as thirty men and women who earned their living by buying and selling 'Palace secrets'. In November 1959 Mr. George Murray, the acting chairman of the Press Council, speaking in Bonn to an audience of journalists and parliamentarians, said that British newspapers naturally sought every possible scrap of information about the royal family, but that the Queen and her family were entitled to their privacy, and there were limits of tolerance on press publicity. In days of high-speed cameras and television, this divergence of interest presented an almost impossible problem, but with the aid of an additional press secretary at Buckingham Palace with practical knowledge of newspapers, he thought there had been a 'distinct improvement'.

Commander Colville's aims may have been laudable. He seems to have lacked subtlety and he has shown an inadequate understanding of Fleet Street psychology. Newspapermen are instructed to satisfy an apparently insatiable public thirst for royal news. The sure way to get bad publicity in popular newspapers is to behave to correspondents in a 'superior' manner. This in itself is an incentive to unkind reporting.

The main cause of trouble, when the Press Council again in 1957 referred to bad relations between Fleet Street and the Palace, was the Palace's inept handling of the strange episode of Group Captain Townsend's visit for the purpose of winning Princess Margaret's hand. Just why the Princess did not arrange to confine their meetings to the privacy of visits to any of the great houses where they were welcome guests, has not been adequately explained; it seems probable that she intended their much publicized meetings to end in marriage, but found the difficulties too great. What is clear is that the immense publicity given to every moment of their courtship was damaging to royal prestige. No one doubts the popularity of Princess Margaret and the sincerity of public sympathy in her

PICTORIAL

May 31, 1959 ✦ ✦ ✦ No. 2,302 Fourpence
THE NEWSPAPER FOR THE YOUNG IN HEART

19-day-old baby drama

WHERE is MY BABY? These four words from a frantic twenty-one-year-old mother started a dramatic hunt in Derby yesterday.

For the baby who vanished, Elizabeth David Bradley, is only NINETEEN DAYS old. And she was on the run for a week.

For two hours, the tension grew.

Then little Elizabeth was found, in the home of Mrs Bradley, of Douglas-street, a very few minutes' walk from Derby. But then she came out of the store Elizabeth and the pram had vanished.

Elizabeth was left in her pram outside a store in Victoria-street, Derby, while

her mother, Mrs. Maureen Bradley, was shopping. Last night a woman was taken to the police station.

A STUPID INSULT

THE strip cartoon reproduced above comes from an American magazine published in New York.

The cartoon—entitled "Bringing Up Bonnie Prince Charlie"—is no doubt intended to be smart and funny. WE SAY THAT IT IS A CHEAP AND CONTEMPTIBLE INSULT. Copies of the magazine with its tasteless strip cartoon are unfortunately circulating in Canada.

A Canadian reader was so disgusted he sent it to the Pictorial with this comment: "I feel that if you published this in your paper, enough people would complain to the magazine in question and discourage them from making further insults on the Royal Family."

We have our doubts whether the American publishers of this muck will be influenced by appeals to their sense of decency. We are certainly not going to publicise the magazine by giving its name.

Reproduced by courtesy of the Sunday Pictorial, 31 May 1959 dilemma was real, but the result of so much familiarity was to produce not contempt for her personally but to wide questioning of the whole business of royal publicity. In point of fact, as Mr. Malcolm Muggeridge pointed out in a much discussed article entitled 'Royal Soap Opera': 'The application of film star techniques to representatives of a monarchical institution is liable to have, in the long run, disastrous consequences. The film star soon passes into oblivion. She has her moment and then it is all over. And even her moment depends on being able to do superlatively well whatever the public expects of her. Members of the royal family are in an entirely different situation. Their role is to symbolize the unity of a nation; to provide an element of continuity in a necessary changing society.'ᵍ In short, what goes for Rita Hayworth merely deprives the Monarchy of dignity.

Mr. Muggeridge's strongest point was that all these speculations about the Princess's future and her motives in inviting Group Captain Townsend to England and rejecting his suit could have been avoided by any sensible press officer. A plain, frank explanation of the situation would have satisfied the public, while pompous and evasive bulletins could lead only to 'an orgy of vulgar and sentimental speculation', and, Mr. Muggeridge suggested, even to the growth of republican sentiment in the minds of serious people. He saw in the new attitude to the Monarchy the effort to create an *ersatz* religion, which would not stand up to reality. 'As a religion, monarchy has always been a failure; a God-King invariably gets eaten. Men can only remain sane by esteeming what is mortal for its mortality.' He added (though not in print) that 'some people thought that they could use the Monarchy as an ace of trumps to use against Communism. If it ever were so used, it would turn out to be the two of clubs.'

Mr. Muggeridge might have written in even stronger terms if his article had appeared during the preparations for Princess Margaret's wedding. Everyone enjoyed the spectacle, and many rejoiced in the fact that a royal princess in direct line of succession had married a commoner and one who was seriously concerned with contemporary artistic development—a matter in which the royal family has not been interested since the death of George IV. Unhappily, the whole affair was smeared over with ribaldry; nor could the press be blamed for laughing at Buckingham Palace's singular ineptitude in the matter of the 'second best man'.

Another of the Queen's critics, Lord Altrincham, made similar criticisms of the Queen's performances on the platform and at the microphone, complained of her 'tweedy entourage' and the narrow outlook of her official advisers. He held that she could have far more contact with representatives from the Commonwealth nations, brown, yellow and black as well as white. Lord Altrincham, who, ironically enough, is a romantic and indeed a passionate monarchist, was struck in the street by an infuriated patriot. His picture of the ideal monarchy seems in some essentials closely to resemble that rather vaguely conceived by Edward VIII. The Monarchy may still, he believes, play a powerful role in unifying the Commonwealth by regular periods of residence in its various capitals. The Queen should show the width of her sympathies not merely by select lunches to which a few respectable writers and intellectuals are invited, but by keeping in personal touch with Asian and African personalities. He argues that the Monarchy can still today maintain dignity and respect and even an aura of romance, provided it totally dissociates itself from the tradition that makes it the head of the aristocracy in a class society.[h]

Lord Altrincham is demanding a social revolution, since Britain is today a class society and the influences that make the Monarchy its apex are still apparently impregnably entrenched. The unity of the Commonwealth again exists, in so far as it may be said still to be a reality, as a matter of convenience; it no longer depends on common allegiance to the Crown. India, Pakistan, Ceylon and Ghana are all republics; South Africa has left the Commonwealth and Malaya has maintained its indigenous monarchy. The Queen cannot be fair to all her Dominions; she cannot divide her time proportionately in each Commonwealth nation. The greatest success of her reign so far has been her 1961 visit to India, where, as in her American tour, she was visiting an independent country which no longer has chips on its shoulder and is untroubled by any of the political undercurrents which were unavoidable in Canada and Australia. Neither in India nor America was she received as Queen or as a symbol of unity. In these countries because she was there as a welcome guest—and special glamour still belongs to a queen—she could be herself, and a very agreeable self Indians and Americans found it. In India she was remarkably uninhibited; naturally flattered by the colossal crowds that everywhere greeted her, she responded with a spontaneous gaiety that she has seldom shown in this country. She repeated her success in Ghana.

I have in front of me a mass of newspaper cuttings which show only too clearly what happened on some other tours. From Australia and Canada I read official claims that the royal tours were a triumphant success, side by side with complaints from less exalted quarters that the Queen and the Duke were not allowed to visit ordinary people, who would have liked to welcome them happily and familiarly as they do other respected and popular visitors. The 1959 tour of Canada was widely regarded as a lamentable contrast with the earlier visit of the royal pair before the Buckingham Palace Press Department had cast its shadow before them.

Here in the Dominions, as in Britain, the Monarchy was unhappily making the worst of two worlds. George V achieved immense popularity, but he never descended from the throne. That epoch is over. The choice was clear enough. The royal family could have maintained its dignity and the Monarch performed her functions as chief magistrate by living simply and unaffectedly among ordinary people as Scandinavian royalties do. The alternative was a garish publicity in which the royal family was known, not frankly as other officials are known and judged, but as the strange beings from Hollywood are known to TV viewers and readers of Sunday papers. They are subjects of gossip and speculation; their costumes, their daily habits, their courtships (real and fictitious), their quarrels and reconciliations are regular and sometimes slanderous newspaper sensations.

The story of Princess Margaret illustrates the result of

The rare, the rather awful visits of Albert Edward, Prince of Wales, to Windsor Castle, by Max Beerbohm

Courtesy of William Heinemann, Ltd.

Dons of Magdalen at great pains to incur no imputation of flunkeyism by Max Beerbohm

Courtesy of William Heinemann, Ltd.

Reproduced by courtesy of the Sunday Express, *21 January 1962 and* The Spectator, *19 January 1962*

trying to enjoy the popularity of stardom while clinging to the unearned privileges of royalty. The Princess's marriage to a commoner was a welcome concession to modernity, but the effect was nullified when he accepted a title. People could over-look the extravagance of their honeymoon on the royal yacht and only began to grumble when they took half the first-class seats on an aircraft to avoid the common contacts of man-kind. Again, in aristocratic circles it is not unusual to leave a two-month-old baby in the care of nurses while the parents fly to the West Indies. But working women have been taught to regard the royal family as a model of domesticity and think that they would never have done such a thing themselves. Mr. Armstrong-Jones's wish to continue his career as a top-class photographer was welcome, but few would defend his decision to devote his talents, not to a national cause, but to boosting the circulation of a commercial Tory newspaper. And should the public be asked to contribute to the internal decoration of Princess Margaret's home, when she is a rich woman in her own right and in receipt of an unearned salary from the State of £15,000 a year? For the first time for a century the royal family in 1962 has been the subject of cartoons and caricatures. Popular newspapers have dared to call her conduct 'perverse and petulant' and, with an irony that recalls popular criticism in an earlier period of royalty, have suggested that if Lord Snowdon could work for the *Sunday Times*, Princess Margaret might join the *Mirror* as woman's editor, the Queen Mother supply 'recipes for bannocks' and Prince Philip sign on with *The Yachting World.*[j]

If Monarchy still had any magic attached to it, it has now been stripped away with a vengeance, and, so, alack, has too much of the respect which should surely be paid to important public servants, as long as we think it necessary to maintain them.

7

THE COST OF MONARCHY

THE cost of the Crown is discussed, always inconclusively, in the House of Commons at the accession of each new sovereign. The occasion cannot be escaped because legally each new monarch makes a bargain with the Government; it owns Crown Lands which it surrenders in exchange for the Civil List.

The sum voted for the Queen's salary and expenses is called the Civil List because, after experience of Stuart rule 300 years ago, Parliament was no longer willing for the King to pay for and control the fighting services. Until then, the Monarchy, which meant, in effect, the Government as well as the royal estate, had been expected to live 'of its own', that is, on the revenues of its own property, aided from time to time by special votes for which the King came to Parliament. It was because kings needed additional money to run the country and its wars that Parliament established its ascendancy and that Britain became a constitutional monarchy at a time when most countries were still arbitrarily governed. When William III arrived from Holland a new system began. The King was to pay for the Civil Service, foreign ambassadors and judges, not for the military establishment. For these purposes he was granted £700,000 annually, and it was not until 1820 that a special part of the Civil List was earmarked for the King's personal expenditure. The £60,000 granted to George IV for his own use out of a Civil List of £850,000 did not, of course, prevent him falling deeply into debt. All Hanoverian kings spent far more than Parliament offered them; they and their courts were grossly corrupt and extravagant. Parliament had met George I's debts by an additional grant of £1,300,000 and had voted sums of £513,511 and £618,340 to cover George III's exceptional expense account; much of it was spent on bribery and the creation of King's Friends within Parliament itself. During the eighteenth century Parliament had also become accustomed to voting annual sums of about £2,000,000 for the purposes of government.[a]

With William IV a more business-like system was introduced, and the Civil List assumed the form in which it is presented to Parliament today. A bargain is struck between the Parliament and the new Monarch. The vast properties which legally belong to the Crown are exchanged for the Civil List. On his accession the Monarch 'owns' some of the most profitable properties in central London, including Regent's Park and much of the area round it, most of Regent Street and lower Regent Street, Carlton House Terrace and other immensely valuable property in the Mayfair, Piccadilly and Whitehall areas, in the City and West End, in Outer London and on the South Coast, as well as in Ascot, Windsor and other parts of the Home Counties. At his accession the Monarch owns about 150,000 acres of English agricultural land scattered about the country, 105,000 acres, mainly moorland, in Scotland, 1,000 acres in Wales, much of the foreshore round the British coast and the bed of the sea which produces revenue 'from the right to take sand and gravel, from jettys, from oyster beds, and (in Scotland) from salmon fishing'. Apart from large investments in Government stocks, the Sovereign surrenders a large number of antique rights from which her predecessors once drew revenue. They include wrecks, estrays ('any beast not wild, found within any lordship, not owned by any man'), various legal fines and forfeits, excise duties on beer and wine licences, temporalities of bishoprics during vacancy, treasure trove and other oddments.[b]

In exchange for the revenues from these properties, Edward VII received a Civil List of £470,000 and George V £410,000. The List is divided into four categories—Her Majesty's Privy Purse, Household Salaries, Household Expenses and Royal Bounties, alms etc. Queen Elizabeth's list, voted in 1952,

was £475,000, which included a supplementary provision of
£95,000, designed to insure the Crown against the danger of
inflation. £25,000 of this was to be available to provide for
members of the royal family who are not ordinarily in a position
to earn their own living. About £100,000 was diverted from the
Duchy of Cornwall's revenues for the future expenses of Prince
Charles. He would receive the total revenue of the Duchy when
he reached the age of twenty-one; £30,000 would be yearly
devoted to his use between the ages of eighteen and twenty-one.
£60,000 from the Civil List was regarded as necessary for the
Queen's personal needs and an extra £40,000 was taken from
the Consolidated Fund for the Duke of Edinburgh.

The long debate in the House of Commons on 9 July 1952
was really a mixture of two debates. One was on the official
Opposition's amendments, and the other on what was really
the republican issue, whose most effective speaker was Mr.
Emrys Hughes. Mr. Attlee's amendments dealt with the need
of more Parliamentary control; why not a review of royal
expenditure every ten years? Again, was not the provision for
Prince Charles excessive and, as many Members asked, was it
not absurd to decide then and there what might be paid to the
widow of a child of three years old? Other Members asked
why it was necessary to decide Princess Margaret's grant on
marriage without waiting to know how rich her future husband
might be. And, if you were insuring the Queen against the risk
of inflation to the tune of £95,000, what about the 180 impover-
ished and distinguished persons who received in tiny allotments
a total sum of £2,500 from the Civil List? (The Government's
only concession was to consider altering the ceiling here to
£5,000.)

One Member wanted to know the constitutional duties of
the Duke of Edinburgh before giving him £40,000 a year.
Mr. Butler, the Government's spokesman, was on this point as
evasive as his predecessors had been about Prince Albert. Mr.
Hugh Gaitskell wanted to rationalize the Civil List: couldn't a
much larger part of it be put under some departmental vote?
But Mr. Butler would have none of it. If too large a part of the
royal income were controlled in this way, it would 'take the

heart out of what is in our British Monarchy a personal house-hold'. As for periodically reviewing their expenditure, that would be a bad thing, disturbing to the happy relations between Parliament and the Crown.

Most Labour Members would have been content with small concessions. They felt that any criticism of the Monarchy was in bad taste as well as bad electioneering; monarchy was undoubtedly an expensive luxury, but, they argued, an elected president might interfere more with Labour policies than a constitutional monarch. The most practical reformer was Mr. John Parker, once Secretary of the Fabian Society. In a speech which infuriated some of the Tories, who thought all forthright discussion of the Queen's income indelicate and unpatriotic, he argued that the House should know the size of the royal family's income before deciding how much more its members needed to enable them to do their job. Monarchy, he said, was accepted in England as a convenient way of running the country, but it must be modernized. All revenues from the Duchy of Cornwall should go to the Treasury; palaces, whose upkeep was included in the Civil List, should be put under the Ministry of Works; it was absurd for the Palace of Westminster, for instance, to be partly in the care of the Ministry and partly of the Queen. The House should know what 'alms' were included in the Queen's vote—did the phrase mean that she still gave to the nationalized hospitals? Why must the Queen have thirty-five ceremonial horses; should there not be 'a pool' of horses, as there was a pool of ceremonial cars? Why should not junior royalty be allowed to earn their living like other people; and why shouldn't royal persons be paid salaries like other public servants?

Fun in the debate came from Mr. Emrys Hughes who proposed to reduce the Queen's £475,000 to £250,000 and to cut the Duke's allotment to £10,000. He pointed out that the Queen of Holland seemed comfortable enough on £14,000 for herself, £28,000 for Prince Bernhard and £33,000 for the up-keep of the one royal palace that she had not passed over to the nation. He proclaimed himself a republican 'like President Eisenhower'. He described the List as 'the largest wage claim

in the country'. He told the Tories that when they 'are demanding a scrutiny of the expenditure of the nationalized industries
they should demand economy in our oldest nationalized
industry'.

The House of Commons always cherishes at least one
licensed jester, and Mr. Hughes, who is usually well informed
as well as witty, remained persistently popular. After all, he
could not be dangerous; only twenty-five Members supported
the proposal to reduce the Civil List and fifty-six voted to cut
the Duke's salary. In the debate he was supported by Mr. Cahir
Healy, a Republican from Northern Ireland, who said what he
basically objected to was that 'too many people surrounded
the Sovereign and cost too much'. He didn't agree with his
numerous colleagues who kept saying how much they liked
ceremonies which embodied the traditions of England. On the
contrary, 'the more primitive people are, the more they demand
ceremonial'. Other M.P.s from industrial areas asked how these
large sums spent on the Monarchy would look to their working-
class constituents. They did not hate the royal family. On the
contrary they had great respect for Queen Mary. She was a
dignified old lady, but they were puzzled to know why she
needed £70,000 a year. This was a hit nearer home than they
realized, for Queen Mary was in fact immensely rich. No one
answered Mr. Parker's question about the size of the royal
family's private incomes.

It will be seen from this debate that discussion was limited
to the categories under which the Queen's income was divided
and there was no discussion, in spite of Mr. Parker's questions,
about the interesting details on which journalists love to
speculate and which readers of Sunday papers tirelessly read.
Indeed, the subject of royal finance is a carefully maintained
mystery. The reason, for instance, why Commonwealth
countries are not encouraged to contribute to the upkeep of
the royal family—except for sharing in the cost of entertaining
it on royal tours and perhaps providing the Queen with a
house—is that they would have the right to make enquiries
about the Civil List if they contributed to it. Ministers and
Palace officials divulge no detailed information; the excuse is

that it would involve prying into the Queen's private affairs. But then what is private and what is public?

Does the Queen pay income tax? We know that monarchy pays no death duties and it is for that reason that the great riches of the royal family have increased from reign to reign. Articles have appeared, in usually reliable papers, stating that the Queen is the only person in Britain who pays no tax at all. This appears to be a mistake. According to the Palace itself, the Queen pays income tax on some portions of her property; on Sandringham for instance, which was built by Albert when he had sufficiently developed the royal income from the Duchy of Cornwall. It is now estimated to be worth about £3,000,000. Since we do not know in any detail what part of the Queen's property is subject to tax, this information does not really help. How much, for instance, are these royal residences, which are the personal property of the Crown—the Queen has several, apart from Balmoral and Sandringham—taxable in the normal sense? In view of the large part of their upkeep which falls on the Ministry of Works, it must be a problem to calculate the expense allowances accepted by the income tax authorities. Again, the Queen has very large private investments; they presumably are taxed like other people's. Some apparently well-informed writers state that George VI voluntarily paid income tax and assume that Queen Elizabeth does the same. A curious incident occurred in 1959, when the Inland Revenue authorities proposed to tax the profits from some Derbyshire lead mines which belong to the Queen as part of the Duchy of Lancaster. The suggestion was described (by whom?) as 'out of the question' and withdrawn. So presumably the Duchy of Lancaster, which brings her in an income of about £100,000 a year, is not taxable, though it is not included in the Civil List.

Inquisitive citizens constantly ask where the money comes from to pay for the marvellous dresses which the Queen wears on ceremonial occasions. Such questions are considered rude and when the answer is, very naturally, that they are paid for out of the Privy Purse, it is easily assumed that this means that she 'pays for them herself'—which is true provided we remember that the Privy Purse is part of the Civil List voted by

Parliament. Any full enquiry into the mysteries of the Queen's expenditure is considered dangerous; it might lead to a serious proposal that the State should take over the Duchy of Lancaster, the Duchy of Cornwall and other properties which are not included in the Crown Lands. If that were done, the Queen might be paid a salary like other public servants. She might be reduced, as one commentator remarked, to the position of the King of Denmark, who now gets £145,000 a year—subject to variation with the cost of living, like the wages of some trade unionists.

The truth is that we are all supposed to like a romantic and traditional haze round the Crown. What would journalists do if, in ignorance, they could not speculate about the Queen's 'housekeeping problem'? They solemnly discuss whether she can make ends meet in view of the increased cost of laundry and food. Forty families, we are told, reside within the royal mews and the Queen has to supply the servants who live there with an annual suit of clothes. There is good journalists' material in the fact that the common mute swan holds a unique position in Britain as a royal bird and that 'although anyone may keep swans as captives on his own private waters, and if they escape may pursue and recapture them provided the pursuit be continuous, all others at liberty on open and common waters belong to the Crown by prerogative right'.[c] Grants of swan-rights used to be made by the Crown, however, the owners marking the cygnets at the annual 'swan-upping', and the two City Companies, the Dyers and Vintners, have exercised their rights on the Thames continuously from the fifteenth century to the present day. Miss Laird tells us, among other fascinating details, that the Queen receives silken flags each year from the Duke of Wellington 'as quit rent for Stratfield Saye and one fleur-de-lys from the Duke of Marlborough for Blenheim Palace'. I long to know what has happened to these flags; is the same one used every year, or are they stowed away in a storeroom at Windsor Castle? The Queen has other traditional obligations. She pays £3 to each mother of triplets, makes a present of £27 annually to the Poet Laureate (whose total salary is £99 a year), and she is apparently entitled to a

Photo: Sport and General

Happy at Ascot

Unhappy at Badminton. This was reproduced on the front page of the *Sunday Pictorial* on 28 April 1957, with arrows pointing at the Queen and Prince Philip at the opposite ends of the row, and with a query whether Prince Philip did not seem 'Odd Man Out', explaining that he was bored with the Queen's passion for horses and horse-racing

Photo: Daily Mirror Library

Photo: London Express News and Features Servic

The Long Lens: father and son at Cowes

A Quiet Courtship: Group Captain Townsend

Photo: Daily Mirror Librar

crimson rose from the Duke of Argyll, which, one gathers, she seldom gets. All whales and sturgeons that come to our shores are her property and on Maundy Thursday and at Christmas and Easter she bestows gifts on the aged poor and aids the education of children whose fathers have been killed in the armed services. She subscribes to many charities and provides London hospitals with daffodils from the royal gardens.

This is the picturesque side of royalty. There has been much rivalry in English and American magazines to estimate the size of the Queen's private fortune. One American magazine guesses £54,000,000 and calculates that she is the third richest woman in the world. Lord David Cecil makes it £10,000,000. He is clearly not including her unique collection of pictures and furniture. He may have forgotten that she possesses five tons of gold plate. Her pictures alone were valued at £15,000,000 in 1958; 2,000 of them are presumed to be old masters. They cannot be regarded as personal property in the full sense, since she could not, in practice, dispose of them even if she desired. There would certainly be an outcry if she sent a couple of Rembrandts to be sold at Christies. It has been reasonably suggested that the Queen's pictures, now in Windsor, Buckingham Palace, St. James's Palace and elsewhere, should be shown in a gallery always open to the public.

The value of the Queen's furniture and objects of art cannot be estimated; seventy-five large volumes are needed to catalogue these valuables at Windsor. She also owns the most remarkable and precious collection of jewelry in the world. It includes scores of items whose exact pedigree is known, and whose value depends as much on their history and association as on the magnificence of the stones. She has the world's most famous collection of stamps. George V devoted three afternoons a week to their care and when told that 'some fool had paid several thousand pounds for a stamp', merrily replied that he was that fool. Other sources of the Queen's private income, apart from those derived from the Duchies of Lancaster and Cornwall, no doubt include large investments; on these financial matters the Crown has been well advised. Sir Edward Cassel was valuable to Edward VII as a financial consultant as well as a friend. All this omits the huge private fortune he inherited. In 1889 it was officially admitted that Queen Victoria had saved £824,000 from the Civil List during her retirement; and an eccentric, named John Nield, left her another half a million pounds. She owned at least £2,000,000 when she died. Much of this has come down to Queen Elizabeth and it should be noted that Queen Mary left £406,000. It would seem, all in all, that the estimate of Queen Elizabeth's private fortune as £50,000,000 to £60,000,000 may be well within the mark.

The usual Palace handout, which has been useful to innumerable journalists and popular writers, is that the Monarchy is really very cheap indeed, even in strictly financial terms, since the Treasury receives a net annual income of more than £1,000,000 from the Crown Lands, which is more than it pays out in the Civil List. This maintains the legal fiction that a large part of central London, as well as all the other properties surrendered at the accession, really 'belonged' to the Queen when they were surrendered. It also totally omits large sums of expenditure on royalty which are included in the Army, Navy, Air and Civil Estimates.

Public attention has fastened on the cost of the royal yacht *Britannia*, which was fitted out for about £2,000,000 and cost the public £7,000 a week when in service and £4,000 a week when stationary. This goes in wages for twenty officers and 237 ratings, and seems not to include the cost of fuel. It can be argued, and often is, that this is not excessive, because to hire other suitable forms of sea transport would also be very expensive; that except on special occasions, such as the honeymoon trip of Princess Margaret and Mr. Armstrong-Jones, the yacht is used only for official tours when the Queen and Duke must show the flag in royal splendour; and that anyway the yacht is so fitted that it can be swiftly transformed into a hospital in time of war. The cost is borne by the Navy, which is asked to regard it as a useful supplementary training ship. The Air Estimates include provision for the Queen's Flight; similarly, the constant ceremonial use of the Brigade of Guards and Household Cavalry in the Queen's personal service is accounted for in the Army Estimates. Other indirect expenses appear in the Civil Estimates; the Ministry of Works, for instance, pays for the running costs of a number of royal residences. Some of these expenses would, of course, be incurred under any system of government. Just how much more we pay for them in a monarchical system than we should pay in a republic, no one can guess.

This is the strange part of the story. No one can say what the Monarchy costs, since its finances are still confused with those of government. The pageantry and trappings of royalty are obviously expensive, but a fiction is maintained that they cost the nation less than nothing because the Crown owns property that, in everything but law, belongs to the State. The Queen earns a salary and an expense account. Why should she not be properly paid like other public servants? The muddle and secrecy about royal finances is indefensible; it springs from the mist of antiquity and pretence with which the institution of monarchy is enveloped. The accepted argument in its favour is that we like its magic and value its traditions. But we really ought not to pretend that we do not pay for these hallowed survivals.

8

PRIVATE SECRETARY TO
THE SOVEREIGN

IT WAS NOT UNTIL 1861, when Queen Victoria was left a widow, distraught with grief, and obviously unable to cope with her own correspondence, that the office of Private Secretary to the Sovereign was officially recognized. The pretence was maintained that Secretaries of State were the only secretaries that the Monarch needed; Parliament protested against the appointment of a personal secretary to George III, even when he was blind and often demented, and it would give no constitutional sanction to similar appointments made by George IV and William IV. During the early part of her reign Queen Victoria did without a private secretary. She took advice from Lord Melbourne and Baron Stockmar and after her marriage, of course, relied on the Prince Consort. After his death she made use of the services of General Grey who had been Albert's Private Secretary. The first officially recognized Private Secretary was Sir Henry Ponsonby; he was appointed in 1870 and, though he was necessarily the repository of every state secret, he was not made a Privy Councillor until ten years later. Sir Arthur Bigge, who succeeded Sir Henry, put the office on to a business basis, and when Sir Frederick Ponsonby was appointed an Assistant Private Secretary to Edward VII on his accession, he found that there was a staff, some of whom even knew shorthand and typewriting.[a] Today Sir Michael Adeane, the present Private Secretary, has two assistant private secretaries, a press secretary with an assistant, a chief clerk, a secretary to the Private Secretary and eight clerks.

144

That the British Monarchy survived its conflicts with advancing democracy was due in no small measure to the fact that this office, almost unknown to the public until recently, was in its testing time held by patient and adroit diplomats. The Private Secretary to the Sovereign is one of the most influential of public servants.

The publication of Sir Henry Ponsonby's *Life and Letters* by his second son, Arthur Ponsonby, revealed for the first time how great a strain Queen Victoria imposed on everyone who served her. Sir Henry himself could scarcely have endured her service had he not possessed a keen sense of the ridiculous. In his diaries and letters to his wife, he was able to let off steam about the Queen's obstinacy, prejudices, selfishness and partisanship. His most illuminating letters were written from Balmoral, to which weary ministers were constantly forced to travel under conditions of great discomfort and to the grave embarrassment of public business. The Queen complained vehemently of any attempt to persuade her to alter by a day a schedule which she imposed without any thought for the needs of government or the convenience of ministers. They wanted to kill her, she declared, if they asked her to stay within reach rather than delay some important matter of public business which no one dared to suggest could be transacted without her constitutional approval.

King George V's behaviour during the 1931 crisis provides an impressive contrast. King George had planned to go to Balmoral on the night of Friday, 21 August. In view of the Cabinet crisis he suggested to MacDonald that he should postpone his departure. The Premier, fearing that a change in the King's plans would increase the panic, advised him to go as arranged. Early next morning, when the King had only just reached Balmoral, a telephone message warned him that his presence might soon be needed in London. He declared that it was 'no use shilly-shallying on an occasion like this', and returned to London the same night.[b]

The brunt of Queen Victoria's unreasonableness was naturally borne by Sir Henry Ponsonby. He chafed—with a humour that yet included some bitterness—at the months he was compelled to spend at Balmoral, separated from his wife, shivering in its vast unheated rooms, intolerably bored by its meaningless waiting and fantastic discipline. He remarked that there could really be no parallel for a court in which the Queen spent most of her time in a remote fastness, and yet kept so strict an eye on her servitors that none of them was allowed to go for as much as a walk until she had herself left the castle. There was no conversation, and for ministers and guests mainly nothing to do. Sir Henry Campbell-Bannerman wrote to his wife: 'It is the funniest life conceivable. We meet at meals and when we are finished each is off to his cell.'c

One of Sir Henry's tasks was to convey to ministers the wishes of the Queen even when they were wishes that, as Monarch, she had no business to express. He contrived to do so with such discretion that it was not until their correspondence was published, many years later, that the world discovered how tyrannical the Queen was in private, and how willingly she would have been tyrannical in public life too if native prudence and a wise Private Secretary had not come to her rescue. The fat would indeed have been in the fire if Mr. Gladstone's radical supporters had known that she told Sir Henry to make it plain that Mr. Bright and Mr. Chamberlain could not 'remain in the Cabinet if they again attacked the House of Lords'. Ponsonby, in obeying her instructions to inform Gladstone of her views on Bright and Chamberlain, added: 'But I certainly think with you that it might scarcely be desirable to repeat these remarks to these two ministers.' Joseph Chamberlain never learnt that she described him as a 'socialist', and Lord Rosebery, who had married a Rothschild heiress with an income of £100,000 a year, would have been surprised if Sir Henry had informed him that the Queen thought that one of his speeches was 'radical to a degree to be almost communistic'.

Sir Henry's way of managing the Queen was not Disraeli's. He strove to be sincere, even though he had to disguise his thoughts. He would have preferred not to be so diplomatic. It was his duty to save the Queen from herself and to maintain the personal confidence of ministers even when, as in the case of Disraeli, he had little sympathy with their politics or their methods. In confidence he wrote that Disraeli was 'most clever. But he seems to me always to speak in a burlesque. All the time I saw him about the crisis I could scarcely help smiling. In fact I think him cleverer than Gladstone with his terrible earnestness. But how anyone can put faith in Dizzy is what I don't understand.'[d]

Yet even Dizzy respected him and paid tribute to the fairness of the bowdlerized versions of the Queen's instructions that he passed on to ministers. Being an honest man of liberal sympathies, Sir Henry could not wholly hide from the Queen that he did not share her enthusiasm about Disraeli's foreign policy; in private, he said, with precise insight, that she saw the issue as a personal battle between the Tsar and herself for the leadership of Europe. She was not satisfied when Ponsonby suppressed his own opinions. She demanded his active agreement and sympathy, and in 1877, at the height of the Turko-Russian crisis, telegraphed to the Dean of Windsor to come to Buckingham Palace so that he might convey to Sir Henry her regret that he was not more in agreement with her about the eastern question, and did not more sympathize with her fury about Mr. Gladstone's policy. The Dean came and did his best to carry out her instructions—much to his own and Ponsonby's embarrassment.[e]

In general, Sir Henry avoided open disagreement with the Queen. He never made the mistake of arguing with her. The only result of opposing her views was that she refused to discuss the matter further with her adviser. Arthur Ponsonby gives some telling illustrations of his father's technique. Thus Sir Henry wrote:

'The Queen asked me who could represent her [at the funeral of the Empress of Russia]. . . . I said, the Duke of Edinburgh. The Queen said, "No, of course, he couldn't." I said, "Of course he couldn't." But I did not know why, I got back to him in the course of conversation and said it was a pity he couldn't. So she telegraphed to him to ask him if he could and he said he would.'

The Queen's correspondence abounds in examples of Sir Henry's ingenuity. Arthur Ponsonby chooses the example of a letter she instructed his father to write in reply to one by Sir Garnet Wolseley who had just won a military victory against the Zulus. In describing this Sir Garnet referred to an army reform which he believed had been favoured by the Prince Consort. The Queen described this letter as 'A shameless and shameful letter', and instructed Sir Henry, without one word of congratulation on Wolseley's victory, to say that the proposed changes would have been highly disapproved by the Prince Consort. Sir Henry's letter contained the congratulations which the Queen failed to offer and added that Sir Garnet's references to the Prince Consort's views 'did not meet with the Queen's entire approval'. This, as Arthur Ponsonby remarked, is a notable example of the conveyance of a royal admonition in a letter of warm appreciation.[f]

After Sir Henry's death in 1895, Sir Arthur Bigge (later Lord Stamfordham) was appointed. Though he was the son of a clergyman in Northumberland and not appointed through the usual Establishment channels, Bigge, like all the royal private secretaries, had the training and experience of a soldier. He had been a close friend of the Prince Imperial, and was entrusted with the task of bringing back his body when he was killed in the Zulu War in 1869. This involved an interview with the Queen; she was so much impressed with him that she appointed him a Groom-in-Waiting, put him in charge of the arrangements for the Princess Eugenie's visit to South Africa and made him Assistant Private Secretary on his return. When Edward VII came to the throne he had his own confidential secretary in Lord Knollys, and Bigge became secretary to the Duke of York, who, in 1910, became King George V. King George retained both Knollys and Bigge. As we have seen in the story of the House of Lords crisis, it was a matter of real importance that the King accepted the advice of Knollys to the outspoken anger of Sir Arthur Bigge. Knollys, like Sir Henry Ponsonby, was a Liberal in sympathy and it was because he was too 'political', that is, too Liberal, that he retired in 1913.[g] The King always felt aggrieved that Knollys had failed to report Balfour's readiness to form a government if the King had refused Asquith's request for a contingent guarantee to create peers.

From 1913 onwards Stamfordham played a constitutional role which may well have been as important as that of Sir Henry Ponsonby. Like the King he was a high Tory, but was always cautious and correct in dealing with Liberal ministers. Their friendship was deep and sincere; to no one else did George V open his heart so frankly; to no one else did he express the same affection and gratitude. When he died the King wrote to Princess Alice that he was 'the most loyal friend he ever had'. Stamfordham's confidant was Randall Davidson, who was as conservative an archbishop as the King or Stamfordham could have desired. Stamfordham was annoyed when told that he kept criticisms from the King, and indeed there is no reason to believe that he was ever anything but frank and outspoken in his relations with him; both Asquith and Ramsay MacDonald paid tribute to his impartial aid in times of crisis. It was Stamfordham, the King declared, who 'taught him to be a King'. He could warn and even scold the King (in respectful terms, of course) and when he did so King George was willing to listen with humility—a rare virtue anywhere, particularly uncommon with kings.

Stamfordham certainly advised him wisely when he had to choose between Baldwin and Curzon, and he helped him to maintain a scrupulously correct attitude when, to his alarm, it became clear that Labour governments were unavoidable in 1924 and 1929.[h]

Stamfordham died in the spring of 1931 and it was, therefore, his successor, Sir Clive Wigram, who advised the King during the crisis that led to the formation of a National Government and the continued premiership of Ramsay MacDonald. Sir Clive's memoranda make it abundantly clear that the King exercised a decisive personal influence in bringing together the leaders of the three parties and forming the National Government. George V had by that time acquired great experience and achieved the self-reliance that he lacked in the pre-war House of Lords and Ulster crises.

At no time, of course, did George V ever present his Private Secretary with a problem similar to that which faced Lord Hardinge when he was Private Secretary to Edward VIII. As the Duke of Windsor readily admits, his Private Secretary was doing no more than his duty in warning his master that a Cabinet crisis was impending as the result of his relations with Mrs. Simpson. He was, however, hurt by the 'cold formality with which so personal a matter affecting my whole happiness had been broached'.¹ What no doubt most shocked and hurt the King was his secretary's blunt proposal that 'the only one step which holds out any prospect of avoiding this dangerous situation' was for Mrs. Simpson 'to go abroad without *further delay*'. The King interpreted this advice as, in effect, an indirect message from Mr. Baldwin, and it does indeed seem improbable that Lord Hardinge would have ventured to make such a suggestion without prompting from the Premier.

The instance stands alone in the history of royal private secretaries, in that an official, whose loyalty is solely to the King, was in this case required to speak for the Cabinet. The Private Secretary's right to give the King friendly and personal advice was used in this case by the Premier, who could not in the sphere of the King's private life tender 'advice' in the technical sense which the King must constitutionally accept.

It is only recently that professors and other students of English institutions have awakened to the importance of the Sovereign's Private Secretary. The fullest comments so far to appear on this subject are to be found in an appendix to Wheeler-Bennett's *Life of George VI*. He quotes, with approval, Professor Laski's eloquent review of Ponsonby's life of his father and explicitly endorses his striking comment that the relations of the Private Secretary to the King are similar to those which (in Walter Bagehot's oft-quoted words) should be followed by the Sovereign in his relation to his ministers. Just as the King has 'the right to be consulted, the right to encourage and the right to warn', so the Private Secretary may expect to be consulted by the King and to encourage or warn him about his constitutional behaviour. Wheeler-Bennett finally points out that the Private Secretary has long been largely responsible for maintaining the Crown as 'a dignified emollient' in our Constitution, but today is becoming far more important since, with the emergence of the new Commonwealth, 'the private secretaries become the sole link between the sovereign and her Governors-General overseas', and between Her Majesty and her Prime Ministers throughout the Commonwealth. As Sir John Wheeler-Bennett puts it, he 'must shape the whisper to the throne', as it is spoken in Ottawa, Canberra, Wellington, Columbia and Accra, as well as in England. 'All have equal access to their Sovereign and the channel of that access is the office of the Private Secretary.'[j]

The Sovereign's Private Secretary stands at the very heart of the Establishment.

9

THE EDUCATION OF PRINCES

IN BETWEEN the lists of battles won by Britain in foreign parts Victorian school histories used to summarize the characters of our kings and queens. They were good or bad. Sometimes the label referred to their private morals; sometimes to their political achievements. King John, for instance, was described in one book as 'desperately wicked with more than ordinary wickedness'. Henry VIII was good because he gave us a navy, and bad because six wives is too many. These historians failed to point out that a good king was apt to be followed by a bad heir; the son of a monarch who lived in conjugal bliss was inclined to take full advantage of the opportunities of promiscuous pleasure that his position so profusely offered. Thus, to go no further back, the gay monarch was the son of the pious Charles I; George III, always domesticated even when insane, followed his heavily amorous grandfather, George II. George IV, again, was the most notorious of libertines. Victoria started and sustained a new era of royal and national prudery. Edward VII revived the tradition of pleasure-loving monarchs. His son, George V, returned to the simple austerity of his grandmother. Edward VIII's revolt against convention could have been prophesied. George VI restored the broken image, but the usual alternation has not followed his reign. He was succeeded by a daughter whom no one is likely to accuse of being anything but a pillar of propriety.

If this alternation is not invariable, neither is it accidental. It is the natural product of the education of princes. Prevented by their exalted status from mixing with other children, they have lived secluded lives, been taught and supervised by private tutors and governesses, often strictly disciplined in youth, only suddenly to be released into a world of unparalleled opportunity and no responsibility. Like other adolescents, they have commonly rebelled against their parents' way of life; their fathers, having crowns to preserve, have tended to be even more than commonly jealous of their parental authority. They have viewed with marked distaste the rival establishments that inevitably grow up round the heir to the throne. Even in modern England, where we have outlived political assassination and wars of succession, the emancipated heir to the throne is likely to be surrounded by rich people who have failed to make the grade at court. Princes, like their parents, live in a closed and yet much publicized world; their lives are highly artificial and their activities are ceaselessly photographed. The press, the films and television manufacture for them a public *persona* which may or may not bear any close resemblance to the truth. Their smiles or their sulks are matters of comment in a million homes. They are likely to choose friends who will court favour by administering to their whims, while basking in the glory that is reflected from everything royal.

The task of educating the royal heir and harnessing his, perhaps, wayward fancies to the restricted life that is to be his, has been tackled in a variety of ways by reigning monarchs—but seldom successfully. The usual problem of adjustment between parents and adolescent children is exaggerated in their case by the princes' knowledge that the inheritance is in any case theirs; they know, like Prince Hal, that if they are to have a good time it must be while they are young; the time will inevitably come when the gilded cage of fictitious power will close round them. When that happens, whether they have behaved themselves or not, their mothers and sisters and aunts will curtsey to them. They may have to wait for middle-age or they may find themselves chained to a throne before pleasure or suffering has taught them anything. But the future is certain; it has not to be earned.

The story of Edward VII's education by Albert and Victoria needs no retelling. We understand why he 'burst into tears'

when on his seventeenth birthday he was presented with a
lengthy 'moving document' which began: 'Life is composed
of duties . . .'. As a boy the most striking concession made to
pleasure or modernity was when some sprigs of the aristocracy,
boys of his own age at Eton, were asked to come to the Palace
to tea. Even his courtly biographer admits that the presence of
Prince Albert on these occasions tended to damp their festive
character.[a] Albert's code of education for the heir to the
throne was simple; it left no time for sport or relaxation, since
the morning, afternoon and evening had to be devoted to books.
The one tutor Edward liked, the Rev. Henry Birch, was taken
from him, much to his childish distress, apparently because
Birch had won his affection and did not give an adequate report
of his faults. Colonel the Hon. Robert Bruce, who took his
place, was a disciplinarian, specially recommended for
'decorum', but neither he nor the two tutors who looked after
Edward when he was at last allowed an independent establishment at Richmond ever succeeded in interesting him in books.
Short periods of residence at the universities of Edinburgh,
Oxford and Cambridge equally failed to inspire the Prince
with a love of academic learning. Though on Albert's instructions many hours every week were devoted to memory
training, Edward remembered nothing at any time of his life
except what served his purpose; he remembered people, gossip
and the score. The truth about him was discovered by the
British Ambassador in Constantinople, who wrote after
Edward's visit there: 'I do not think he will study much or
learn much from books, but he will attain all that is practically
necessary for him to know by observation and use it with
address.' No summary could have been more prophetic. As
King, Edward did very nicely on what he learnt from conversation, more especially from female conversation. He never saw
any reason to agree with his father that life was composed of
duties; on the contrary, he found that it passed very agreeably
in a perpetual round of pleasures.

      To Queen Victoria nothing he did was right; if he amused
himself she upbraided him. Her worst suspicions of the friends
he chose were confirmed when they led him into the baccarat

scandal and the divorce court. She never regarded racing as a sport fit for kings. 'I fear, dear Mama,' he wrote at the age of twenty-eight, 'that no year goes round without your giving me a jobation on the subject of racing.' If he showed a desire to take his position seriously, she was no better pleased. She said it was unconstitutional for him to know secrets of State, and dangerous, too, since he was addicted to untrustworthy society and could not possibly be discreet. He was always the naughty boy who had given trouble to Albert. It was on a visit to Cambridge occasioned by his wayward behaviour that Albert had caught the cold that led to his final illness. For this she bitterly blamed him. Moreover, he was in every respect the opposite of Albert, and that was enough.

When George V came to the throne he was scarcely more trained for his job than Edward VII had been, though the strict discipline of life as a naval officer led in this case to behaviour which was the reverse of his father's. He had not been born to the throne. His elder brother, Prince Eddie who, fortunately for the British Monarchy, died before his father, was a dissolute and unintelligent young man who caused his family great anxiety. The fact that such embarrassing heirs occur at unpredictable intervals in royal family trees is one of the strong arguments against hereditary monarchy. His parents' idea of saving the throne from disgrace was to find a hard-headed, sensible wife, who would see to it that decorum at least was observed during a reign which could not in any case be very creditable. They chose Princess May of Teck. She fulfilled all the specifications: when Prince Eddie died her affections, after a decorous interval of mourning, were luckily found to be transferable to his brother George. Later, as Queen Mary, she became popular with the British public; and as her correspondence with George V shows, a marriage of convenience turned into a partnership of affection. George V, a modest, shy and timid man, who hated any interruption of a routine which gave him a sense of security and adequacy, found this dominant and unimaginative woman precisely the wife for whom he would have prayed. She did not worry him with cultural interests which he found merely boring; she put up with the poky little house which he decorated according to his own philistine taste; she was even more deeply conservative than he—conservative in way of life, in social obligations, as well as in politics. Queen Mary in fact did much to atone for George V's lack of training for his job, and she rescued him from the embarrassment of Queen Alexandra's possessive and unwise affection. She was herself possessive in another way. She had a genuine love of antique furniture and some expert knowledge in this field. People who possessed beautiful things that she coveted seem to have lacked the courage to refuse to give them to her. The pain of loss was no doubt offset by the prestige of making gifts to Her Majesty. Queen Mary's greed may be dismissed as a royal foible. What is hard to forgive is her treatment of her eldest son since his abdication. That she should be deeply upset at his behaviour is intelligible enough, but that she should never receive his wife, even as much as to give her a cup of tea, seems outside the character of normal motherhood.

Neither George nor Mary developed even the rudiments of commonsense when it came to the education of their children. George was a martinet. Like his father, he was passionately concerned and minutely informed about every detail of uniform and all the protocol of dress. He sent a rebuke to Lord Birkenhead when he saw a photograph of him in the press arriving at 10 Downing Street in a lounge suit and soft hat and he thought it 'rude' of Birkenhead to reply to his Private Secretary that 'in days far more formal than ours it was never the custom to appraise the adequacy or dignity of Lord Chancellors in terms of head gear'. He could spot and deeply resent a misplaced button on the uniform of any British regimental uniform, and he applied the same type of criticism to his children. Margot Oxford once told me how she was with George V when his elder son came into the royal presence in a knickerbocker suit. He was sternly ordered out of the room to change his clothes and report to his father properly dressed. She ventured to remonstrate with the King about the un- wisdom of so wounding a sensitive boy in front of visitors. The story has been related that Lord Derby at a later date suggested to George V, who was his guest, that the King might cultivate the friendship of his sons; he himself had gained so much happiness from the affection and intimacy of his children. George V replied: 'My father was frightened of his mother; I was frightened of my father, and I am damned well going to see to it that my children are frightened of me.'[b]

His oldest son, called David in the family, and destined for a few months to be King of England, has described his childhood in what is probably the most illuminating book ever written about the education of princes. He was psychologically in revolt from the first—from the time when, almost a baby, he was regularly brought to his parents in tears because a sadistic nurse pinched him. It is a strange reflection on George and Mary that it was months before they discovered that their son was crying from pain, not from a rebellious nature. He was a sensitive child, who quickly understood the feelings of his misfit tutor whom he once discovered looking wistfully out to the free view beyond the Palace gardens. He hated cricket, but wanted to be with other children. Even at Oxford he was surrounded by perpetually interfering tutors. The 1914 war was his first opportunity. He wanted to share dangers like other young men and he felt for a few brief months the happiness of being 'a proper chap' amongst fellow officers who treated him as an equal with a job to do.

After the war he found the Palace as intolerable as he had as a child; the only difference was that his father no longer summoned him to his study to rebuke him for some reported peccadillo. In those days the only relief had been holidays at Sandringham with his indulgent grandfather who took his side against governesses and tutors, and who seemed, as he recalls in retrospect, to have offered a life 'bathed in perpetual sunlight'. Now, released by the war, his father's routine, 'fixed like a planet in its orbit', 'moving with precision at precisely the same time every year from one royal residence to another', was completely intolerable. He loathed the vast *battus* in which his father found his highest pleasure. It was of no interest to him that on a single day 2,000 brace of pheasants or partridge could be entered in the royal game-book. He detested the 'musty smell of Buckingham Palace'. He saw one outlet. His father had one, and only one, original idea. Whereas Edward VII had belonged to the old tradition of our Hanoverian dynasty and been interested in the courtly politics of petty German princelings as well as in the entanglements of the European balance of power, George V was passionately attached to the Empire, and at first approved his eldest's son's desire to become acquainted with it. Edward VIII saw in the wide open spaces under British rule a chance of freedom and self-expression. He became, as the newspapers irreverently put it, Britain's travelling salesman. His father, unable to disapprove, was constantly alarmed and astonished at David's restlessness.

When after the First World War Edward, then Prince of Wales, visited India he was given stern instructions by his father. George V had vivid memories of the Durbar of 1911; it was a magnificent ceremonial occasion which brought him into no contact at all with the Indian people. He warned Edward that in visiting 'the brightest jewel in the imperial crown', he must not indulge in any of those informalities which had brought him so much popularity in Canada and Australia. The King had disapproved of them in the White Dominions, but in India they could not be countenanced. Thus, he told the Prince, he must do exactly 'as they tell him'. Edward correctly interpreted 'they' as meaning the British civil and military authorities in India. As a result of their advice his visits to towns like Bombay and Calcutta turned into a race on the part of these authorities to outstrip the Congress *hartal*, which, they explained to the Prince, was due to Gandhi's 'intimidation'. They even told him that the food which it was customary on such occasions to distribute to the Indian poor was rejected because Congress had started a rumour that it was poisoned.

When he left India the Prince was at least aware that he had not been in touch with Indian realities. He knew that polo, royal processions and tiger shooting with maharajahs were no longer the things that mattered. He was to find, he said, as more than one traveller had before him, that 'the truths about

India are elusive. She remained a mystery, fleetingly perceived through an interposed layer of British officialdom and princely autocracy—crowds of natives cordoned off by troops and police, and toiling figures in endless fields seen from the window of my train.'c

When he came to the throne he was in a muddle, which was the result of many factors, the chief of which was his education. But he had done much to educate himself, and it could be said that when he ascended the throne he was, in the matter of understanding world events, more nearly fitted for it than any British monarch in modern times had ever been.

King George's second son, Albert, destined to take his brother's place as George VI, suffered even more than his elder brother from his parents' utter incapacity to understand their children. As the Duke of Windsor remarks, their father successfully hid his affection from them, treated them like unruly midshipmen under naval discipline and, in fact, loved his children 'in the abstract', rather than in the particular. Queen Mary did nothing to interfere, though she seems to have occasionally remonstrated with her husband when he seemed unnecessarily severe. If Edward was pinched by his nurse, Albert suffered no less by her neglect. The two princes were happy with her successor, and got on well enough with Finch, an apparently sensible fellow who looked after them as small boys. But the appointment of Mr. Hansell, who chose a staff of tutors under him to take charge of the boys' education, was even more disastrous for Albert than for Edward.

George VI has not, like his brother, written about his own childhood, but his biographer has revealed the essentials. Whereas David was a bright, spirited child who beneath the surface was always on the edge of revolt, George was a timid, slow-minded boy, who was reduced to stammering misery by his father's frequent rebukes. Like the Prince Consort, whose notion of a birthday greeting had been a formally written memorandum on the duty of obedience, the Duke of York wrote to him when he was five years old about the advantages of learning early to be obedient. 'I always tried to do this,' wrote his father, 'when I was your age.' Things grew worse

under the tutelage of Mr. Hansell. He was appointed because
he was a scholar of indubitably correct opinions, good at
games, a crack shot and an expert yachtsman. To do him
justice, he saw that the boys ought to be sent to school; when
he suggested this to their father he was rebuffed. The boys
should be brought up as far as possible in the same way as
their father; they must not mix with ordinary children. The
Navy would complete an education begun by private tutors.
Mr. Hansell did his best to create the atmosphere and the
conditions of a public school. Indeed, Wheeler-Bennett writes:

> 'Mr. Hansell's principal defect, however, was one of
> excessive virtue, and the virtue of his period and back-
> ground. He might, in fact, have stepped straight out of the
> pages of one of Dean Farrar's great school romances. His
> was the muscular Christianity of *St. Winifred's*, and this
> might not have occasioned too great a difficulty had he not
> have expected his pupils to be equally imbued with the
> characteristics of *Eric, or Little by Little*. This they most
> certainly were not. They were quite ordinary little boys
> with no more of original sin about them than any others of
> their age and weight, but equally with no more outstanding
> virtues than their contemporaries.'[d]

And Wheeler-Bennett then reveals the unhappy secret of
'a series of leather-bound notebooks containing the weekly,
and sometimes daily, reports of Mr. Hansell' on the progress
and conduct of the boys. They make shocking reading today.
'Both boys must give a *readier* obedience'. They were not
getting on with their arithmetic; one little boy had tried to
kick another, and so forth. Each of these disgraceful revela-
tions was followed by a summons to the Library, so graphically
described by the Duke of Windsor, where in the coldest terms
their father admonished and warned. Albert made so little
progress in his studies that it was only with difficulty that he
was accepted at Osborne and at the Royal Naval College. He
was often at the bottom of the form. It was considered a
triumph when he came sixty-third out of sixty-eight. At

Dartmouth he discovered some of the joys of companionship and was even flogged with sixteen other boys of his own age with the Navy's traditional severity and publicity. Unlike David, however, he found compensation for his inner conflicts and unhappiness, not through revolt, but through religion. Perhaps he was most genuinely happy when mingling on easy terms with boys in camp life. Parental influence won the day, and he became as nearly as possible a replica of his father. Marriage to a confident and socially gifted woman finally made public life possible for him.

No such psychological problems appear to have troubled the life of the present Queen. No experiments were made in her education or in that of her sister Margaret. Many details of her childhood and education have been revealed in unnecessary, but no doubt lucrative, detail by their governess, Crawfie. A more authoritative account is given by Mr. Morrah, who explains that the children were educated according to 'a clearly conceived plan, which was framed by their mother. By comparison with the curricula of the leading girls' schools of that day or this, the plan would be considered somewhat old-fashioned; indeed, Queen Mary, who was by temperament more inclined than her daughter-in-law to put a high value on strictly intellectual discipline, sometimes expressed her misgivings.' But the Duchess of York 'pursued her course, untroubled by other people's doubts'. The children were to be in the open air as much as possible. They were to learn to love country life. This appears to mean they were to find pleasure in racing and riding; the Queen is excellent on horse-back. The princesses were 'to acquire good manners and perfect deportment and to cultivate all the distinctly feminine graces'. It was also desirable for them 'to develop a civilized appreciation of the arts, and especially of music', and to 'gain as much reasonable book learning as might prove to be within their capacity'. But when it became apparent 'that Princess Elizabeth would never progress beyond the simplest elements of mathematics, it did not worry the Duchess at all'.[e] There was after all no necessity for Elizabeth II to become a bluestocking like Elizabeth I, who mastered five languages as a child, and could converse fluently in any one of them with archbishops or ambassadors.

Princess Elizabeth learnt French, but, unlike all her Hanoverian ancestors, failed to master German. From the Provost of Eton she learnt what an heir to the British throne must know about English history, especially constitutional history, and the working of our institutions. Towards the end of the war she had a brief period of serving in uniform and, like other girls of eighteen, got dirty learning about the inside of a motor-car. She ascended the throne with very much the dutiful and highly conservative outlook on life which she had learnt from her mother, but it must be added that she was not lucky enough to learn the secret of an easy, smiling, personal aplomb which made the Queen Mother a social success. Elizabeth's marriage with Prince Philip was exactly what was expected of the Queen of England. Princess Margaret, gayer and more lively in disposition, found affairs of the heart less simple. She was not the sort of girl to marry one of the numerous minor royalties who are out of work on the Continent. The marriage she contemplated with Group Captain Townsend was abandoned. It would have involved, as Edward's marriage with Mrs. Simpson involved, a breach with the Church of England's prohibition of marriage with divorced persons—a rule frequently overlooked—and therefore possible only if she, too, forfeited the dignities and position attached to royalty. Mr. Armstrong-Jones, though a commoner and a member of a much divorced family, was eligible as a husband for the most eligible bride in Europe.

It is clear that Elizabeth and Philip have thought very seriously about the problem of their children's education. They had too much understanding of the world around them and too clear a warning from the past to think it possible that their son Charles should be brought up in all the ignorance of private tuition. What were the alternatives?

The problem of royal education is certainly difficult. How can a child grow into a normal adult if the national anthem is played in his honour and headlines announce every stage of his progress with more emphasis than they give to the deaths of a thousand people in a battle or a famine? How is he to grow up in a sensible relation with other boys if his first jolly experience of kicking a football is photographed on ten million newspaper pages?

In none of the Duke of Edinburgh's skirmishes with the press does he so unreservedly deserve public support as when he attempts to preserve his children from being prematurely involved in royal glamour. One applauds his anger when a load of press photographers at Cowes followed the boat in which he was teaching his son how to sail. On one occasion, defending himself against the charge of rudeness to the press, he is reported to have said that he certainly is 'bloody nasty to the photographer who pokes his long lens through the key-hole into my private life'. Special requests were made to the press to prevent such ambitious photographers from taking photographs of Charles from outside the walls of his school. On two occasions Commander Colville issued appeals to the press to allow Prince Charles to grow up outside the glare of publicity. There have been lapses in some newspapers, but on the whole this appeal for decency has been successful.

It will probably be agreed that the heir to the throne need not be a scholar; that modern languages will be useful to him, that he needs a general understanding of the world and a special knowledge of the Commonwealth. He needs to grow up with a modest idea of his own position and qualities, and to avoid the fantastic snobbery which, so far in the history of monarchy, has always surrounded the Court. From an early age he knows that he belongs to the most exclusive and privileged club in the world; he knows, even as a schoolboy, that the day will come when none of the elders and betters of his youth will question his opinions or criticize his actions. This problem is one of the most difficult that the upholders of hereditary monarchy have to meet. A president is chosen for this position because he is held by his countrymen to possess some at least of the qualities required for high office. A king—we note the accident that Prince Eddie did not become King—may have none of these. Indeed the very fact of being born into the purple makes it less likely that a prince will ever be qualified to be King.

  Brave suggestions for the solution of this problem of the Prince's education have not been lacking. The Queen and the Duke have had plenty of advice on this matter and it has come from many quarters. Herbert Morrison (Lord Morrison of Lambeth) has argued that the best solution would be to send the Prince to an ordinary county school, 'moving onward by examination and scholarship to higher education at the University'. Even if he may not have the advantages of the ordinary rough-and-tumble with other boys of the middle and working classes, he should certainly not go 'to Eton or to any other establishment, however excellent in itself, where he is likely to make exclusive friendships with the future leaders of one political party'. Would not the King be better qualified if he had mixed as a child with other ordinary children?

  Lord Altrincham, whose father was at one time equerry to Edward VIII when he was Prince of Wales, is an aristocrat who despises the conception of hereditary aristocracy. But his advice about Prince Charles's education is not basically very different from Lord Morrison's. Of the Queen, who disappointed him by failing to emancipate herself from her conventional role in a class society, he writes: 'Will she have the wisdom to give her children an education very different from her own? Will she, above all, wish to see that Prince Charles is equipped with all the knowledge he can absorb without injury to his health, and that he mixes during his formative years with children who will one day be bus drivers, dockers, engineers—not merely with future landowners or stockbrokers?' Passionately believing that the Monarchy should be the unifying factor in a disintegrating Commonwealth, Lord Altrincham wants the Prince to grow up equally at home in India, Canada, Ghana, Australia and London. Eton, where he was himself educated, he regarded as the worst possible school for the Prince; at Eton, he argued, he would be surrounded by boys sent there mainly because of their money or because their parents are the kind of snobs who want their children to belong to a particular kind of élite. His main contention is that monarchy cannot last if it remains the pinnacle of a class hierarchy. A class society, he believes, is doomed in any case. The Monarchy may survive and play a unique and saving role if it rises above class and welcomes the new type of society which is struggling to be born.

Lord Altrincham's concept of monarchy is no doubt romantic, and Lord Morrison's will be thought unrealistic. In the end a decision has been made to send Prince Charles to Gordonstoun, where the Duke of Edinburgh was himself educated. This does not meet all the critics' requirements. Gordonstoun is no doubt an upper-class establishment. But it is an unusual school. It is not like Eton, which has become somewhat unfairly a popular synonym for aristocratic privilege and jumped-up commercialism, often chosen by parents because it confers prestige on successful products of an affluent society. This reputation clings to Eton in spite of the fact that, like Winchester, it has the highest intellectual as well as snob standards. Charles, who has not shown any special aptitude for books, may not receive as much intellectual stimulus as he might have done at Eton, nor will he rub shoulders with all and sundry as some democrats have wished. But he will not be subject to the snobberies of Eton, and he may learn disciplines that will stand him in good stead.

Kurt Hahn, who, with Winthrop Young, founded Gordon-stoun soon after his expulsion from Nazi Germany, is a man of drive and originality. He has often explained his ideas; they differ from those of Arnold of Rugby. He never believed much in organized games or approved the British cult of athletics. He inspired boys with the belief that if they started to climb a mountain they must get to the top whatever the weather; he taught them that the hardships of sailing in small boats were more worth while than success at cricket or football. As a headmaster, he enforced his own version of 'the honours system' by an eccentric and awe-inspiring personality that was a more than adequate substitute for formal compulsion. He does not himself any longer rule at Gordonstoun; he has been busy starting Outward Bound schools in Holland, Germany, Kenya, Nigeria and Rhodesia. In recent years Gordonstoun appears to have become more conventional than it was in Hahn's day, but it seems clear that his basic ideas have not been forgotten. One of these was that through the daring and courage needed for rescue work in the mountains and at sea, boys may discover what William James described as 'the moral equivalent of war'.

10

MONARCHY'S FUTURE

'*As long as the human heart is strong and the human reason weak, royalty will be strong because it appeals to diffuse feeling, and Republics weak because they appeal to the understanding.*

A secret prerogative is an anomaly—perhaps the greatest of anomalies. That secrecy is, however, essential to the utility of English royalty as it now is. Above all things our royalty is to be reverenced, and if you begin to poke about it you cannot reverence it. When there is a select committee on the Queen, the charm of royalty will be gone. Its mystery is its life. We must not let in daylight upon magic.'—Walter Bagehot: *The English Constitution*

'*In no other western monarchist country in Europe is royalty less democratic, so widely separated from the people, so aloof, so profoundly snobbish socially as in this politically most democratic of all countries. In a Stockholm park, one might come across a tall, spare gentleman who would greet one cordially and even stop to talk; later, one might learn that this was King Gustav of Sweden. When he was younger, King Christian of Denmark was often to be seen mingling with the crowds in the streets of Copenhagen. . . . In England such things are unthinkable. Not that royalty does not make an honest effort to meet the people and even to mingle with them at the numerous layings of corner-stones, unveilings of monuments and opening of fairs and charity bazaars. But there is always an air of artificiality about these royal meetings with the people; there is a taste of slumming about them. Royalty performs a "job" in coming among the people and no one is allowed to forget for a moment the presence of H.R.H. the Duke, or H.R.H. the Duchess. There is*

167

a stiffness about the relationship of British royalty and the people which smacks of Germany, whence, of course, it hails direct.'—*The Twilight of the British Monarchy*, by an American Resident[a]

THE rationalist view of monarchy can be stated like this: In a pre-scientific age society is ruled by magic, not by statistics; weather prophecy is a matter of imperfect personal observation, not of scientific precision reported by the B.B.C.; crops respond to dancing and sacrifice, not to artificial manure; famine, pestilences, hurricanes, earthquakes and volcanic eruptions are signs of divine wrath and cattle plague is due to the evil eye. In such a society it is reasonable to bow down to kings or priest-kings who rule, punish, reward, mediate and reassure. Periodically the king must die and a virgin king succeed him. Sometimes, if the weather is disobliging, the crops fail, or the national armies prove unsuccessful, the king, having failed to fit the expected pattern, may be sacrificed, unceremoniously pushed off the throne or sent to govern the Bahamas.

In these remote and superstitious ages the king's friends, whose power and prestige depend on royal favour, are naturally anxious to preserve the doctrine of divine right, or, when that theory has to be abandoned, to maintain as far as possible the magical illusion, which still gives powerful and irrational support to the crown. With the growth of science and democracy, people begin to realize that monarchy is a survival, surrounded by superstitions which must be outgrown along with haunted houses, being thirteen at table and the disastrous effect of walking under ladders. An ideological battle is then joined in which the ruling class, whose position depends on retaining the existing social structure, use all the resources of propaganda to persuade the uneducated and the half-educated that in some mysterious way the monarchy is still sacrosanct and essential to the safety of the realm.

This is a summary of the traditional republican case which is now seldom stated in blunt terms because monarchy no longer lays itself open to criticism on grounds of private vice or political interference. The argument that the Crown is expensive and unnecessary still crops up, but it is rare to find an angry young man willing to incur unpopularity by an attack on monarchy as an institution. H. G. Wells was still an angry young man at eighty. As late as December 1944, when he was nearing his death, he sought an opportunity of restating his republican faith. He wrote: 'I have always regarded and written of monarchy as a profoundly corrupting influence upon our national life, imposing an intricate snobbishness on our dominant classes, upon our religions, educational, military, naval and combatant services generally, burking the promotion of capable men and reserving power in the community entirely for the privileged supporters of our Hanoverian monarchy.'[b]

Mr. Leonard Woolf has also described monarchy as a debilitating survival from an irrational past, deliberately maintained in the interests of privilege. In *Quack Quack* he wrote that there had been a chance that we might become civilized, that we might learn to love our country 'because of its physical beauty and its tradition for justice, liberty, intelligence, and culture'. In that case 'the country, the King, and the people would all be civilized. It was against this danger that the ruling classes and the people reacted vigorously.' The public attitude to the Monarchy, he continues, has changed 'because an intense propaganda by public men, in the press, and in the cinema, has been carried on day after day for years in order to establish in the people a superstitious "loyalty" towards the royal family'. As a result, an irrational feeling about the whole royal family has been substituted for a sensible respect for the King as chief Civil Servant. Everything is done to decrease the element of rational understanding and to increase the tendency towards magic and worship. A state of mind is created which makes a rational attitude towards all political and social problems increasingly rare and difficult. If our Morris car does not start we do not expect, Mr. Woolf remarks, to make it go by waving flags and muttering incantations over the engine. 'But we teach the children in elementary schools that they cannot be good and loyal Englishmen unless

they approach the more important political questions in the
flag-waving, incantation, medicine-man frame of mind.'

This is one aspect of the case. The growth of a reasonable
attitude has certainly been retarded by the propaganda of
vested interests. That, however, is the beginning, not the end
of the matter. We have to meet fundamental questions that
the nineteenth-century rationalist could brush aside. We may
not believe in original sin, but we delude ourselves if we think
that the phenomena covered by that question-begging dogma
can be disposed of by simple changes in early training. We may
reasonably look forward to an age when wars no longer
threaten civilization, but we know that they will not be
eradicated merely by suppressing bellicose propaganda in
newspapers or stopping children from playing with tin soldiers.
The sociologist asks us to explain the easy success of anti-
rational propaganda among educated people and we have to
answer those psychologists who deny that our society was ever
on the edge of becoming civilized. We have to consider whether
this desirable society would have come into existence if the
newspapers and the power of government had been in the
hands, not of men like Disraeli and Northcliffe, but of John
Stuart Mill and Sidney Webb. Herbert Spencer, a rationalist if
ever there was one, complained that when we had got rid of
the ape and tiger in man we still had to cope with the donkey.
But the modern sociologist does not consider stupidity the
greatest obstacle to progress; for the donkey he substitutes
the Unconscious. In short, our trouble is that men's reasoning
faculties play only a minor part in controlling the vast iceberg
of irrationality that lies beneath the surface of consciousness.

Consider for the moment the story of Britain in the nineteenth century. After 1832 the middle classes were in the
saddle, and during the vital generation that followed the
Reform Bill they were dominated by the utilitarianism of the
Benthamites. It was indeed taken for granted that, having once
won electoral power and ended the feudal control of Parliament, they would go on to end church establishment and to
abolish all hereditary power, including the House of Lords and
the Monarchy. That this process was checked and less rational

social forces encouraged is certainly partly due to economic factors which transformed Britain into an imperialist nation. But no one could study this period without concluding that institutions which could not be intellectually defended were popularly supported from unconscious motives which reason and argument scarcely touched.

How far can we allow the modern psychologist to push us along this road? Some would totally deny that mankind has ever at any time reached the threshold of a rational society. A quarter of a century ago one of the most orthodox of Freudians wrote to me on this subject. I had written of the magic that still clings to monarchy. He replied that

'Magic really means the feeling-attitudes derived from the unconscious. These are the realities which *cannot be talked away by any sort of so-called enlightenment*. Personally, I think that these unconscious attitudes are much more safely attached to a hereditary monarch whose conduct is pretty well controlled by education and other influences, than being allowed to run loose and up by any particular god of the moment. When Napoleon said that he found the crown in a gutter and picked it up, he was speaking a profound psychological truth and his example was followed more recently in Russia, Italy and Germany, in that order. I do not think the result of this process makes for more sanity than ours.'

It is of course true that in some countries which have become republics, and which seemed ripe for a further stage of democracy, the upshot of a period of crisis has been popular support for a new type of dictator who may inherit some of the attributes of the former monarch. In Germany a wit remarked that if you throw the crown in the gutter some gutter-snipe (or house-painter) picks it up. Yet in Britain we were capable of accepting Winston Churchill as national leader during the greatest of national emergencies; we remained critical throughout the ordeal and rationally decided to discard his leadership at the end of it. Moreover, those who argue that men crave for monarchy and will substitute a dictator if the monarch is deposed, seem to forget that in the great majority of cases where monarchy is overthrown, the result is to substitute an unexciting and perfectly adequate president.

Another psychologist, of a rather different persuasion, with whom I recently discussed this problem, takes a less pessimistic view than my Freudian theorist. He points out that in archaic and tribal societies the masses were—and still are in many parts of the world—comparatively unidentified as individuals; and that in such societies the king is revered or worshipped as the one person who is free to realize his own individuality, unhampered by the taboos and restrictions that are automatically binding on his subjects. Such absolute monarchs are in fact fantasies of infantile omnipotence. From the psychiatric point of view, they are the least developed of personalities since they are given untrammelled power and therefore do not have to relate their own lives to those of others. In short they have the psychology of spoilt children. We need not believe that such autocrats or such subjects are necessary to any part of the human race. There is nothing unscientific in the liberal expectation of a society in which each individual is regarded as separately valuable and given a chance of developing his own personality in association with others. In our society some people cling to the security of the fantasy world and for them the king may still carry the mystique of a person who is free from ordinary restrictions and magically master of his own destiny. But this is not likely to remain a majority fantasy in a scientifically educated world.

We need to know much more about human society before we can assert with certainty that this optimistic view is justified. We do not know, for instance, what proportion of people in any given society are educable in this sense. Indeed we have not seriously attempted to find out, since we still provide higher educational facilities only for a few and leave the majority to the mass propagandists. All we can say with confidence is that some people do attain through education and innate ability an adult capacity for rational judgment about affairs beyond their immediate environment; that this number has greatly increased, especially in the smaller democracies, and that even if the more rational part of the community remains a minority, it seems at least possible that its comparatively rational attitude may everywhere become dominant.

The facts of Scandinavian history, and even of British, seem to support a modified optimism. Walter Bagehot, whose views on monarchy (published in 1867) are still often quoted, would no longer say, if he were alive, that the value of the Monarchy lay in its being 'a disguise' which enables the 'labourer in Somerset' to believe that the Queen personally carries through Acts of Parliament and exercises the functions of government. Today he believes no such thing. Like his working-class friend in Shoreditch, he watches on television when there is a royal show or he may come to London by motor-cycle. He enjoys a jamboree and needs more festivals than he gets. But he does not imagine that the Queen is powerful, and he would be talking rank republicanism in the pub tomorrow if he thought she interfered with government. He is under none of the illusions that Bagehot thought essential or that modern propagandists still assiduously foster today.

If this is true it follows that the symbolic value of the Monarch is not what propaganda pretends. It means that monarchy is no longer psychologically necessary. That does not mean that it need be bad. Symbols may last and be useful provided their content changes. Scandinavian countries have achieved this with marked success. They exist and perform their function without any of the British fuss and bother. King Haakon was elected by the people of Norway, when Norway and Sweden parted company in 1905, and the royal children go to school with the sons and daughters of clerks and labourers. The King of Denmark, who conducts orchestras, also uses the telephone like an ordinary mortal. The Queen of Holland, too, went to college with other girls and was photographed walking arm in arm with them, singing popular songs. When Queen Wilhelmina abdicated after nearly fifty years on the throne she said that 'the Queen is nobody special'.[c] The King of Sweden, himself an archaeologist of repute, is most at home among professors, and recent members of the royal family have been painters and poets. It all seems to work well enough. It might work in Britain.

The case for preferring such a monarch to an elected president has been powerfully made by Dr. Ernest Jones. In 1936 he argued that the problem of government has always turned on 'Man's constantly double attitude towards it'. Men have 'very deep motives for wishing to be ruled'. Feeling unequal to the task of controlling either his own or his neighbour's impulses, he looks to authority to shoulder the responsibility. But as soon as 'the restrictions of authority are felt to be oppressive, he is impelled to protest and to clamour for freedom'. This inner conflict is most obviously expressed in relation to a father-figure. It needs no deep analysis to discover that in adult life men unconsciously regard their rulers as in childhood they have regarded their fathers. They see them as more benevolent or more cruel or more magically powerful than they in fact are, and they feel towards them sometimes an irrational adoration and sometimes an exaggerated hate. Dr. Jones pointed to the remarkable strength of constitutional monarchy which has survived while tsars and kaisers and sultans, who were supposed to be secure, have passed away almost unnoticed. He attributed this partly to the fact that under a constitutional monarchy we are continuously provided with an outlet for both adoration and patricide. In short we can safely accept, respect and love a constitutional monarch, and even treat him as above everyday criticism (rather as we exempt the Speaker of the House from criticism) as long as he strictly confines himself to his constitutional functions. We can do this because at the same time we can attack his ministers and throw them out of office when we please. We do not need to kill the King because, psychologically, we can do so at every general election.[d]

This is to put the matter in a practical perspective. We need not here concern ourselves with the theoretical question whether men can live on a high plane of rationality and through a 'process of so-called enlightenment' rid themselves of unconscious drives and archetypal images. What we have to consider is whether our society can be so organized that this irrationality does not dominate our institutions and our Government. There is no reason to object to fairy stories which help the imagination, or to symbols which aid in understanding the truth. There is no harm in preferring a queen in a gingerbread coach to a president in a motor-car, provided that we know that the family in the coach are like other human beings, civil servants doing a job and being paid a salary for it. We may even find it convenient to treat them with special respect as symbols of national unity, provided that we do not pretend they are more than life size and that the job they do is politically influential and anything more than ceremonial.

A constitutional king and an elected president both have the same two main duties to perform, necessary in any form of society. The first is ceremonial; there must be someone to welcome state guests and to preside on national occasions. The second job, which is of considerable importance in countries where there are more than two Parties, but which will be required occasionally in all nations, is to act as chairman and perhaps negotiator when party difficulties arise, or situations occur which cannot be provided for in written constitutions. On such occasions a sensible king, if we are lucky enough to have one, has certain advantages over a president, because he gains experience through the permanence of his office and he is less open to the charge of partisanship because he is not elected by any of the interested groups.

With the unpretentious George VI on the throne, there seemed a chance that Britian might move towards this type of useful democratic monarchy. The abdication had smashed the taboo; the daylight had been let in. The magic had gone for good and all. In the progressive climate after the war it looked as if the discerning American, whose comments I have already quoted, might be right in saying that the monarchy could no longer remain the 'secret well from which the flourishing institutions of British snobbery has been drawing its nourishment'.[e] This prophecy has not been fulfilled. The Monarchy is still the head of the Establishment rather than the nation; it still represents a social class and apparently still takes for granted, as Lord Esher had carelessly remarked, that it is 'naturally bound to the Tory Party'.

The Palace entourage is still drawn from an exclusive group, mainly from a few families with the tradition of royal service; her servitors are almost all ex-Guards officers and old Etonians; courtiers and visiting Ministers still wear fancy dress and the ladies curtsey as they did to Elizabeth I. Labour and Liberal leaders could legitimately complain to the Queen today, as Mr. Gladstone did eighty years ago to Queen Victoria, that 'the powerful circles in which your Majesty has active or personal intercourse contain hardly any persons who understand the point of view of the majority of the electorate'.

True criticism of the Monarchy today is not in any way personal; nor is it constitutional. It is not financial, though, as we have seen, it is unnecessarily expensive. In the mid-twentieth century it has taken a wrong turning. The Establishment damages it by glorifying it, thus seeking to disguise the power that private persons still exercise over the nation's affairs. The Monarchy could still be respected and indeed loved, as hereditary presidency of the nation and Commonwealth. But if it maintains itself as head of a social class and a vanishing economic order, it can only be a symbol of the past and not become part of the new England that waits to be born.

NOTES

NOTES TO CHAPTER 1

a Dermot Morrah, *The Work of the Queen* (Kimber, 1958).
b Ibid., p. 37.
c The Times, 2 June 1953.
d I owe these and other examples of coronation sentiment to press cuttings collected by Mass Observation.
e Dudley Sommer, *Haldane of Cloan: his life and times 1856–1928* (Allen and Unwin, 1960), pp. 230–1.
f A King's Story: Memoirs of H.R.H. The Duke of Windsor (Cassell, 1951), pp. 278–9.

NOTES TO CHAPTER 2

a Linton's aim was to provide 'at least a known centre and voice' for republicanism, 'to explain republican progress and to establish a republican party in England'. His abstract argument won him few adherents, and he wrote: 'Some few feeble attempts at republican associations of a few working-men, in response to a plan of action from which I looked for results, showed me that I might teach, but might not lead. I stood alone.'

b Harney was devoted to English poetry. But that did not prevent him from saying on Wordsworth's death: 'We are not impressed with any very heavy sense of sorrow. . . . We . . . had no tears for the salaried slaves of Aristocracy and pensioned parasites of Monarchy.' In July 1850 *Democratic Review* expressed its distaste for the fuss made about the birth of Prince Arthur in these terms:

> 'Bring forth the babe in pomp and lace,
> While thousands starve and curse the light;
> But what of that? On royal face
> Shame knows no blush, however slight.
> Bring forth the babe—the nation's moans
> Will ring sweet music in its ear;
> For well we know a people's groans
> To royal ears were always dear.'

c The full story of this incident, and the text of these letters, is to be found in my *Triumph of Lord Palmerston* (Allen and Unwin, 1924), pp. 210–12.

d E. E. P. Tisdall, *Queen Victoria's Private Life* (Jarrolds, 1961).

e The *Beehive* was essentially a trade union paper, not spiced with sex like *Reynolds*, nor intellectual and iconoclastic like Bradlaugh's *National Reformer*. By 1870 it had relinquished its earlier militancy and provided trade union news with occasional political articles, usually on its front page, by Beesly. It discussed monarchy as an institution that needed drastic reform rather than abolition. Beesly defended the Commune and the paper followed the usual working-class line in attacking the annuity to Prince Arthur. But it argued that Dilke was wrong in concentrating on republicanism rather than the reform of social evils. It was loyally sympathetic to the Queen during the illness of the Prince of Wales.

By way of contrast, George Reynolds, who founded *Reynolds News*, was a latter-day Chartist who pioneered in a type of journalism that has proved increasingly lucrative in the twentieth century. It combined sex with radicalism. Reynolds was himself a translator of Victor Hugo and a writer of novels with such titles as *The Seamstress, or the White Slave of England*; *The Loves of the Harem*; *A Tale of Constantinople* and *The Empress Eugénie's Boudoir*. *Reynolds* particularly favoured police court scandals in which the upper classes were involved. It was generally republican in tone and loyal to the Commune. It protested against the 'sickening nonsense' about the Prince of Wales's illness.

f Cf. H. M. Pelling, *The Origins of the Labour Party, 1880–1900* (Macmillan, 1954). He states that the number of such clubs founded between 1871 and 1874 was eighty-four.

g Bradlaugh's own paper, *The National Reformer*, was primarily concerned with militant secularism. In April 1870, however, he wrote describing the private life of George IV as Prince of Wales with obvious asides directed at the private life of Edward, then Prince of Wales. On 18 September *The National Reformer* published a mock report of a commission of enquiry on the seclusion of the Queen, and said: 'A Malthusian (whatever kind of creature that may be) complained that Her Majesty has set an example of uncontrolled fecundity to the nation and the royal family which, besides being generally immoral, is likely at the modest estimate of £6,000 p.a. per royal baby to lead to the utter ruin of the realm in a few generations.' On 26 February 1871 it commended Birmingham's example in setting up a republican club, but warned those who followed it not to be too revolutionary; it would be treason to do anything to shorten the life of the present Monarch, but no treason to agitate for a repeal by Parliament of the Act of Settlement, passed in the reign of Queen Anne.

h Cf. also an interesting, forgotten book entitled *Our New Masters*. It is a study of working-class opinion at the time of the Education Bill of 1870. The author declared that *Reynolds* and the *Beehive* alone represented working-class opinion which was merely another name for utilitarianism. Many working-class people, he said, were not sure that they wanted the Prince of Wales to recover, since the country would be saved £40,000 a year by his death.

Fraser's Magazine (June 1871) claimed that 'For years past republicanism has been spreading among the working-class doctrinally to such a degree that it may be safely said that it is—in some more or less modified form—the political creed of 99 working men in a 100.' An attempt was made at Sheffield to create a National Republican Brotherhood at a meeting of delegates from seventeen clubs. The Brotherhood sought to dissociate republicanism from its connection with the militant atheism of Bradlaugh and Holyoake and to provide a forum for Christian republicans.

i Disraeli's embarrassed explanation of this lapse and the attendant circumstances are recorded in Moneypenny and Buckle, *Life of Disraeli* (John Murray, 1920), Part V, Chapter III, pp. 144–5. Bradlaugh made play of it in his *Impeachment of the House of Brunswick*. 'It is worthy of notice that the Right Honourable Benjamin Disraeli, the leader of the great Conservative Party in this country, publicly declared on September 26th 1871, that her present Majesty, Queen Victoria, was physically and morally incapable of performing her regal functions. One advantage of having the telegraph wires in the hands of Government is shown by the fact that all the telegraphic summaries omitted the momentous words of Disraeli's speech. Benjamin Disraeli has since accepted a peerage from the lady he thus described as morally incapable. During the debate in the session of 1811 it was shown that when the King was mad . . .'

j In 1873 republicanism was given fresh impetus by another royal annuity, this time for Queen Victoria's second son, the Duke of Edinburgh, on his marriage to the Tsar's daughter. A petition was presented for the rejection of the annuity on behalf of 16,000 Northumberland miners. Noting an increase of nine in the number of Members opposing the annuity, *Reynolds* added that it was satisfactory 'to find that even in so rotten a parliament as the present, the feeling against the system of royal cadging is growing apace'. In fact, republican sentiment was not growing, but persisted. J. M. Davidson's *New Book of Kings*, an uncompromisingly republican onslaught on the British Monarchy, first published in 1884, ran to ten editions. In the preface to the tenth edition in 1897 the author said that the fact that the Queen had reigned sixty years must be regarded by every true republican as 'a sort of aggravation of the offence inherent in the Anti-Christ institution of Royalty itself'. In 1887, at the Queen's Jubilee, *Reynolds* remarked that 'Madame Guelph, during her whole reign has been a perfect miracle of energy for the last half century'. Cole and Postgate in *The Common People, 1746–1846*, correctly remark that it was not until the Jubilee that the Monarchy became popular but not, it seems, even then, universally so.

k Keir Hardie: his writings and speeches, ed. Emrys Hughes ('Forward' Printing Co. Ltd., Glasgow, n.d.), Chap. XIII, pp. 61–3.

l Keir Hardie (Allen and Unwin, 1956).

m The Crown and the Cash by Emrys Hughes, M.P., a pamphlet published after the House of Lords debate on the Civil List in 1952.

NOTES TO CHAPTER 3

a Arthur Ponsonby, *Henry Ponsonby, Queen Victoria's Private Secretary: his life from his letters* (Macmillan, 1942), p. 256.

b Christopher Sykes, *Four Studies in Loyalty* (Collins, 1946).

c The Week-End Book (Nonesuch Press, 1924), p. 238.

d As early as 19 March 1907 we find Esher writing to the King that he hears that 'the Cabinet Committee, which is considering the question of the House of Lords, has put aside, in deference to Your Majesty's own wishes, all idea of making proposals which involve touching the hereditary principle upon which that House rests; and have limited their inquiry as to the method by which a serious deadlock between the two Houses is in future to be avoided.' Esher, Vol. II, p. 228.

e Journals and Letters of Reginald, Viscount Esher (Ivor Nicholson and Watson, 1934), 4 vols., Vol. II, pp. 433–4.

f Ibid., Vol. II, p. 457.

g J. A. Spender and Cyril Asquith, *Life of Lord Oxford* (Hutchinson, 1932), Vol. II, p. 25.

h Wheeler-Bennett, *King George VI: his life and reign* (Macmillan, 1958), p. 638. Attlee's reply appeared in *The Observer*, 23 August 1959. Dalton's account is in *The Fateful Years, Memoirs, 1931–45*

(Muller, 1957), pp. 472–5. Herbert Morrison gives a somewhat different account in his *Autobiography* (Odhams, 1960), p. 247. He says that Attlee consulted him on the subject and that his advice was to appoint Bevin as Foreign Secretary. He adds that Whitley, the Chief Whip, agreed with him and that Attlee then agreed too.

i Sir Harold Nicolson, *King George the Fifth: His life and reign* (Constable, 1952), p. 212.

j Ibid., pp. 346–8.

NOTES TO CHAPTER 4

a Dudley Sommer, *Haldane of Cloan*, pp. 391–2.

b Esher, Vol. II, p. 126.

c Ibid., Vol. II, pp. 167–8.

d Sommer, p. 222; also Esher, Vol. II, p. 367.

e Ibid., p. 214.

f Sunday Times, 27 January 1909.

g Robert Blake (editor), *The Private Papers of Douglas Haig, 1914–19* (Eyre and Spottiswoode, 1952), p. 109.

h Ibid., pp. 208–9.

i Hitherto unpublished details of Haig's manœuvres to cover his own share in the futile slaughter of Loos, to get himself appointed C.-in-C. in place of French and to procure his friend, Sir William Robertson, as C.I.G.S. have been revealed by Alan Clark in *The Donkeys* (Hutchinson, 1961).

j On 4 November 1917 Esher wrote in his journal (Vol. IV, p. 152): 'In 1915 the French fought the Battle of Champagne, and in the autumn the Germans took Serbia. In 1916 we fought the Battle of the Somme, driving the Germans back twenty miles. In the autumn the Germans took Roumania. In the spring of 1917 we beat the Germans at Arras, and took Vimy, Messines. The Germans thereupon took Riga and Russia. In the autumn we took Passchendaele; the Germans took Italy.

On one side:	On the other:
Champagne	Serbia
Somme	Roumania
Arras	Russia
Vimy	Italy
Messines	
Passchendaele	

This is how the picture looks.'

a The same view was implicit throughout the nine days' crisis in the columns of the *Yorkshire Post* (where Bishop Blunt's remarks were first printed), in the *Manchester Guardian* and in most of the provincial press. The *Daily Herald* also, in effect, supported Baldwin throughout, basing its attitude on authoritative articles by Professor Laski dealing with the constitutional position. Neither of the opposition parties supported the King's desire for a morganatic solution; Colonel Wedgwood, who moved a Cavalier motion in the House of Commons, spoke, as so often in his highly individualist career, for himself, and not for any considerable body of Labour members. The only daily which espoused the morganatic solution was the *News Chronicle*, which urged that the King had the same right as other people to marry whom he wished, even though the woman of his choice had been twice in the divorce courts and might not be considered a suitable queen. The *New Statesman and Nation* took the same line, pointing out that King Edward's most attractive characteristic was a dislike of humbug which would prevent him making a formal marriage to a royal personage whom he did not love.

b A King's Story, p. 410–11.

a Wheeler-Bennett, pp. 652–3.

b Ibid., p. 703.

c The Twilight of the British Monarchy by an American Resident (Secker and Warburg, 1937), p.23.

d Richard Hoggart, *The Uses of Literacy* (Penguin Edition), pp. 86–7. The whole passage should be read for its careful distinction between the enjoyment of reading the details of the home life of the royal family (super film stars) and loyalty to, or concern with, the institution of monarchy.

e Mass Observation.

f Morrah, p. 99.

g In *New Statesman and Nation*, 22 October 1955. It is significant that the journal in which this article appeared was not flooded with abusive letters, but instead received a number of congratulations for its courage in printing an outspoken and truthful article. Later Mr.

Muggeridge elaborated his argument with some additional and un-flattering references to the Queen's courtiers and to those who instructed her in broadcasting technique. This article appeared in an American paper at the moment when the Queen visited the U.S. It was then that the Establishment exacted its penalty. The excuse for both popular and official abuse of Muggeridge was that he had been personally rude to the Queen.

h Is the Monarchy perfect? by Lord Altrincham and others (Calder, 1958).

i The author of this article was a British journalist with long experience as a foreign correspondent who had been with the royal party throughout the tour. He noted that whereas in 1951 Elizabeth and Philip had been greeted with frantic enthusiasm, in 1959 'perspiring cheerleaders' could, with difficulty, persuade onlookers to 'achieve a little light hand-clapping'. He blamed not the Queen, whom he thought bored, but her publicity staff who offered the journalists only monotonous handouts which, with the best will in the world, they could not build into interesting stories. The tour, he declared, was stripped 'of any flash of inspiration. Almost any town of any size was lobbied for a royal appearance, if only for a few minutes, in order to add its quota of bobbing Aldermen and their wives. Little time has been left for anything else.' The same journalist wrote to me some months later quoting by way of example the excite-ment among journalists when they discovered as a single fact of news that the Queen had been taking shots with a movie camera from the observation car of her train. The public relations mistakes on this tour became notorious; the Duke of Edinburgh's unusual failure with the press on this occasion became world news. The one fact on which everyone agreed was that the Queen and the Duke received a riotous reception in the U.S.

j Daily Mirror, 29 January 1962.

NOTES TO CHAPTER 7

a A convenient summary of this complicated story appears in *Is the Monarchy perfect?* by Lord Altrincham and others, Chapter V: 'The Finances of the Monarchy' by Charles Willcox.

b I owe these picturesque details to Dorothy Laird, whose *How the Queen Reigns* (Hodder and Stoughton, 1959) was, I understand, published after consultation with the Palace authorities.

c Norman F. Ticehurst, *The Mute Swan in England* (Cleaver-Hume Press Ltd, 1957), p. 10.

NOTES TO CHAPTER 8

a Sir Frederick Ponsonby, *Recollections of Three Reigns* (Eyre and Spottiswoode, 1951), p. 102.
b Nicolson, p. 460.
c Arthur Ponsonby, *Henry Ponsonby: His Life and Letters*, p. 124.
d Ibid., p. 244.
e Ibid., p. 163.
f Ibid., p. 224.
g John F. Gore, *King George V: A Personal Memoir* (John Murray, 1941), p. 250.
h The fullest and most appreciative account of Lord Stamfordham is given by Sir Harold Nicolson, *King George V.*
i John Wheeler-Bennett, *King George VI*, Appendix B, p. 823.

NOTES TO CHAPTER 9

a Sir Sidney Lee, *Edward VII* (Macmillan, 1925), Vol. 1, p. 31.
b Randolph Churchill, *Lord Derby: 'King of Lancashire'* (Heinemann, 1960), p. 159.
c *A King's Story*, p. 171.
d Wheeler-Bennett, p. 25.
e Morrah, pp. 16–17.

NOTES TO CHAPTER 10

a *The Twilight of the British Monarchy*, pp. 14–15.
b *New Statesman and Nation*, 23 December 1944.
c Quoted by Lord David Cecil in an interesting article comparing the cost, behaviour and relative stability of 'The Reigning Royalty of Europe', *Life Magazine*, 5 August 1957.
d Dr. Ernest Jones's article originally appeared in the *New Statesman and Nation* and was reprinted in his *Essays in Applied Psycho-Analysis* (Hogarth Press, 1951).
e *The Twilight of the British Monarchy*, p. 39.

INDEX

185